Critical Guides to French Texts

52 Garnier: Les Juifves

Critical Guides to French Texts

EDITED BY ROGER LITTLE, WOLFGANG VAN EMDEN, DAVID WILLIAMS

GARNIER

Les Juifves

Richard Griffiths

Professor of French,
University College, Cardiff

Grant & Cutler Ltd
1986

© Grant & Cutler Ltd
1986
ISBN 0 7293 0238 5

306676

I.S.B.N. 84-599-1113-6

DEPÓSITO LEGAL: V. 2.033 - 1985

Printed in Spain by
Artes Gráficas Soler, S.A., Valencia
for
GRANT & CUTLER LTD
11 BUCKINGHAM STREET, LONDON W.C.2

Contents

For Dominic, Hilary and Katharine

Il pense à ses trois enfants qui en ce moment-ci jouent
    au coin du feu.
Jouent-ils, travaillent-ils, on n'en sait rien.
Avec les enfants.

(Péguy)

Preface

The editions of this play which are most commonly available are those produced by Raymond Lebègue (Belles Lettres, Paris, 1949) and Marcel Hervier (Classiques Garnier, 1945). Both of these are based upon the 1585 edition of the complete *Tragédies* rather than upon the first edition of 1583. This was a sensible choice, as most of the variants (which are rare) are either obvious improvements or the correction of misprints. The only major variant is the excision of four lines (601-04 of the 1583 edition) which were in particularly poor taste; Garnier had obviously had second thoughts.

References in this study are to the Lebègue edition. Readers who are using the 1583 edition (or a modern edition based on it) should bear in mind that, from line 600 onwards, the references will need to be adjusted by the addition of 4 digits.

To appreciate the humanist tragedy of the sixteenth century in France, readers need to take a different approach from that which they have probably taken in relation to drama of other periods. For that reason our first chapter will deal briefly with some general aspects of humanist tragedy, before we turn to the specific characteristics of *Les Juifves*, the greatest example of the genre.

1. Garnier and French Humanist Tragedy

> For the play, I remember, pleased not
> the million: 'twas caviar to the
> general; but it was — as I received it,
> and others, whose judgements in such
> matters cried in the top of mine — an
> excellent play... (*Hamlet*, Act II, Sc.2)

Shakespeare's parody of the tradition of 'rhetorical' tragedy, in the scene between Hamlet and the Players, is as exaggerated as all successful parody has to be; but it is interesting to note that much modern criticism has been equally unfair to French humanist tragedy, which lies within that tradition. By comparing it with the completely different aims and methods of more modern theatre, by looking for 'characterisation', for 'coherent psychology' and for 'dramatic tension', critics have focussed their readers' attention on things which were not even being considered by the playwrights concerned. Viewed on its own merits, the genre is an impressive one, and particularly so in the hands of its most effective exponent, Garnier, whose reputation in his own time was unparalleled, and who inspired imitations and indeed plagiarism right into the seventeenth century. What were these tragedians aiming to do? A positive answer to this will be more effective than any number of negative comparisons.

Unlike the sixteenth-century tragedy of England and Spain, French humanist tragedy was not aimed at the popular market. It followed the Italian tradition of appealing to a minority, consisting mainly of scholars, university audiences, and those members of the nobility who had some education. In part, it was, like the other genres introduced by the Pléiade, an attempt to 'fuyr ce peuple ignorant, peuple ennemy de tout rare, et antique sçauoir', and to 'se contenter de peu de Lecteurs à l'exemple de celuy, qui pour tous auditeurs ne demandoit que

Platon' (*26*, p.181).

One can, however, exaggerate too much this minority appeal. The inflated displays of erudition which mark the poorer playwrights in this tradition are absent from its greatest exponents, Garnier and Montchrestien. In their works, a knowledge of the ancients (and of the Bible) is presumed, and subtle effects are achieved by it; but the knowledge presumed is that of a cultivated Renaissance man, not that of a pedant; and it is worth noting that the plays of both these men *were* eventually performed by popular companies. There is, nevertheless, a long distance from even their plays to the popular theatre of England.

The audience could be presumed to appreciate not only the new treatment of a story they knew well, but also the skilful use which the author made of classical techniques. Mythological references would be understood, quotations and borrowings recognised, variations of the rhetorical forms appreciated.

This theatre was very static; very little in the way of 'action' took place in it, whether physical or psychological. The audience's excitement came from its appreciation of the language used, the themes examined, the interplay between the 'set pieces', the subtle effects achieved by variation, reticence or omission.

One of the most obvious reasons for the static nature of this drama is that it follows ancient tragedy in its lack of detailed examination of the reasons for the tragic event. Where later tragedians (e.g. those of the French seventeenth century) were to be concerned above all with inner psychology, the flaws in character which brought about downfall, and the chain of events which led to it, the humanist tragedian accepted the event as inevitable, and tried to show the effect of it upon his characters. Fate rules this tragedy. In Biblical plays, God takes the place of Fate. At the beginning of a tragedy, the tragic event has either already taken place, or is shown to us as bound to happen. The tragic interest lies in the reaction of mere men and women to this inevitable fate.

The real interests of the humanist tragedians are, however, shown by their choice of classical models. While they spent a great deal of time praising the Greeks, their most constant model was the Roman Seneca. The latter was far closer to their basic literary preoccupations, high among which was the desire to 'illustrate' or 'enlustre' the French language. Seneca provided the stylised framework suitable for such ornamentation; his elaborate rhetorical treatment of tragic themes was far more in tune with Renaissance stylistic needs than was the comparative simplicity of Euripides, Aeschylus or Sophocles.

Current trends in Renaissance rhetoric led to an even more stylised approach than Seneca's. The importance of *progymnasmata*, or model speeches of various kinds, meant that the ideal often became the speech, or the 'set piece', rather than the play as a whole. Formulary rhetoric dealt with separate speeches, either of persuasion or mood, which were separate entities in themselves. Drama tended to become a string of such 'set pieces', often very loosely strung together. Dramatic progression, the realism of dramatic scenes, were sacrificed for an almost operatic technique of solo arias, or of stylised and unrealistic discussion.

Often the achievement was high within these limits, and within the expectations of the audience. Above all, in the greatest playwrights such as Garnier and Montchrestien, these 'set pieces', while remaining formally as separate as within the plays of other writers, contained an interplay of themes, images and tone which created almost a 'drama within the drama', a subtle, coherent and effective way of producing a tragic impact upon the audience.

In all this, one must not forget the importance for Renaissance writers of 'imitation'. They were convinced that, in order to create in their own language a literature which could stand comparison with any other, they must imitate the examples that had come down to them of the two most perfect literatures yet created. Theorists exhorted them to such imitation. Du Bellay's important proviso, however, must be noted. Depicting the Romans as having imitated the Greek authors, he showed them as 'se transformant en eux, et *apres les avoir bien digerez, les convertissant en sang et nouriture*'. Imitation should not be slavish; the classical influence should become transformed by the poet's own invention, become part of the poet's own cultural background, and his imitations should thus become a form of personal expression, rather than prosaic copying.

While slavish imitation *did* exist in much humanist drama, in a play like *Les Juifves* the imitation is much freer; sources are juxtaposed, themes are stressed by detail fed in from diverse sources, the author ranges wide in his variations. Nevertheless, it must be stressed that Garnier's art *rests* on his use of imitation; his greatest effects are reached through it, and would be lost without it.

Use of the Senecan model does not necessarily imply textual imitation of specific Senecan plays. Nevertheless, in *Les Juifves* there are extensive imitations of two Senecan plays; and the interplay and correspondence between these and further imitations from the Bible and Josephus are the basis for some of the finest effects in the play.

Our concentration upon the formal nature of this type of tragedy should not blind us to certain aspects of its content. Donald Stone (*16*) has pointed to the continuity, despite the taking-on of classical forms, of certain medieval attitudes and techniques. It would certainly be wrong to try to stress any kind of formal 'break' between Middle Ages and Renaissance on such matters as imitation, use of *topoi*, of 'flowers of rhetoric' and even of 'set pieces'; a swift look at Curtius's *European Literature and the Latin Middle Ages*, for example, will underline the continuity of literary attitudes, which Renaissance concerns merely adapted. Of equal, if not greater importance is, however, Stone's indication of a mediaeval 'moralising' and didactic tradition which spills over into Renaissance tragedy.

It is possible, of course, to see the concentration on *sententiae*, and on moral discussions, in this type of drama as purely formal and stylistic. There is a great deal, in Renaissance theorists, to support this view, and the practice of certain playwrights would seem to bear it out. There is a danger, however (into which the present writer has fallen in the past; see *4*, pp.96-104), in being too exclusive in such matters. The fact that *sententiae*, and stichomythic discussions, perform a formal purpose does not cut out a moral intent; and the subtitles of Montchrestien's plays, for example, show that a moral 'message' is involved; *Aman ou la Vanité, David ou l'Adultère*, etc.

Religious tragedy lent itself particularly to a general didacticism of this kind. The reason for God's anger, which caused the tragic event, has to be shown. It is clear, however, that this theme was usually expressed in the most general terms, and that the formal discussions within the plays were often taken up with lesser moral themes (rigour versus clemency, suicide versus facing up to one's fate, etc.), treated in a stock manner. Some of these stock arguments, indeed, dealt with moral issues which had relevance to contemporary concerns; but one needs to distinguish these essentially balanced discussions from what Street describes as 'the theatre of sectarian propaganda' (*17*, p.41) — plays written with a propaganda purpose, which often had little formal relationship to 'humanist tragedy'.

French humanist tragedies were performed; many of them were written with performance in mind. For the former, we have historical evidence; for the latter, we sometimes have internal evidence from within the plays themselves (see, e.g., *4*, pp.146-58, 'Stage Representation', Ch.7). The rather unreal controversy which raged at the end of the last century as to whether the plays were performed or not, has long ago been resolved.

The first audiences were at the universities and the court. By the '60s, however, court performances had well-nigh ceased, possibly because of the religious wars, possibly because (according to Brantôme) of Catherine de Medici's superstitious fear of the bad luck tragedy brought. The latter reason is not unlikely; tragedy advertised itself as an 'example', a 'mirror' to kings of the changeability of fortune, and in a time of turmoil kings and queens might well not wish to be so reminded.

Be that as it may, our meagre historical records do not give us much joy in the '60s and '70s; it has been pointed out, moreover, that the tardy publication, during this period, of tragedies that had been written many years before (e.g. those of Jodelle and La Taille), shows the fact that they were originally written for *performance*; but that, conversely, their publication at this stage may have shown the lack of possibility of such performance.

From the mid-'70s onwards, however, a new picture emerges. We have evidence of performance by the *confréries*, and also by professional actors; and, in the provinces, performances at university, or (in the case of Montchrestien) before a local governor.

Our evidence is, however, so slight and fragmentary, as opposed to the wealth of evidence available of performance of contemporary English theatre, that we are forced to presume that such performances were not as common as the authors might have wished. Above all, if the dearth of information for the years 1560-75 means anything (as opposed to a chance lack of evidence), it must mean that authors, even when writing for performance, cannot have been assured of their plays receiving it.

Garnier is one of the playwrights for whom we have the most evidence of performance, from the mid-'70s onwards. Right into the 17th century, *Les Juifves* was performed; Guez de Balzac, for example, informs us that in the neighbourhood of Angoulême a *confrérie* played it every year.

Les Juifves is, too, one of the plays which gives most evidence of having been written with the stage in mind. A technique of importance, in relation to this, is the way in which scenes are linked to each other; the 'justification' for entries and exits; and the impression given of the stage itself being used to create certain effects.

In many humanist tragedies, characters appear to come on and off at will. One can switch from a speech by one character to a speech by another, both of them being monologues, with the audience merely being left to presume that the first speaker is no longer there. Garnier, on the other hand, has two methods of bridging such transitions; 'justification', and the mid-act insertion of a chorus, which will enable people to get on and off stage with no difficulty

Every act in *Les Juifves*, except Act I, has such transitions to deal with. Act II contains a scene between Nabuchodonosor and Nabuzardan, closely followed by a scene with Amital and the Chorus, whom the Queen of Babylon later joins. A Chorus is introduced to bridge the gap. In Act III, the two parts both contain Nabuchodonosor as a protagonist; but the Queen must depart, in order for Amital and the queens to speak with him. The whole thing is very subtly managed, with her giving a reason for so doing. Nabuchodonosor calls for Sédécie to be brought to him; the Queen says she will leave:

> Je ne veux pas l'attendre,
> J'aurois trop de pitié de voir ce pauvre Roy
> Par desastre reduit en si grand desarroy.
>
> (960-62)

Nabuchodonosor is left on stage, with enough time to give us his important monologue; and then, to the audience's surprise, not Sédécie, but Amital, comes on, encouraging her companions to appeal to Nabuchodonosor's pity. We will not see Sédécie till Act IV. The reference to him is therefore a very artificial device; it can serve no conceivable dramatic purpose, other than that of getting the Queen off the stage.

In Act IV, the two major scenes (Nabuchodonosor-Sédécie, and Prévost-Amital-Roynes), which are in two different places, are again separated by a Chorus. In Act V, however, we have another example of two major scenes which need the same person (in this case Le Prophète), but in which his interlocutors have to be changed. In the first scene, he has acted as 'Messenger', to inform Amital and the queens (and the audience); in the second, he takes on his full role as Prophet, in one of the most effective scenes of the play, and in a close dialogue with Sédécie. Amital and her companions have to be removed from the stage. This departure is justified by their need to bury the dead:

> Il faut auparavant que nostre soin procure
> Que les corps trespassez soyent mis en sepulture.
>
> (2063-64)

Again, the transition to the next scene includes a monologue, by Le Prophète.

The skilful use of a wide stage, in this play, is shown by the use to which a common convention of humanist tragedy is put. This is the convention whereby characters are often unaware of the presence of other characters on the stage, so that they speak for a while before addressing them.

The first example of this is when the Queen of Babylon enters in Act II. Amital and the Jewish women have been lamenting. Suddenly the Jewish women see the Queen coming on:

Madame levons-nous, levons-nous, car voici
La Royne avec son train qui s'approche d'ici

(565-66)

The Queen, however, is unaware of them, and launches into her happy *aubade*. The effect is one of a startling tableau; the unhappy Jewish women observing a radiantly happy woman, across the stage. Only at the end of her speech does the Queen notice them: 'Mais qu'est-ce que je voy?' (579).

In Act III the same technique produces a rather different effect. Nabuchodonosor has been indulging in a monologue, when Amital and the queens come on. He *hears* them coming:

Mais qu'est-ce que j'entens? qui sont ces voix plaintives?

(971)

They appear, but do not at first see him. This situation enables certain ironies to emerge from the statements of both Nabuchodonosor and Amital. Only after twelve lines does Amital see him; and even then she calls on God before addressing him directly:

Je le voy: las, mon Dieu, vien et nous favorise,
Inspire nous, mon Dieu, conduy nostre entreprise.

(987-88)

In Act IV, as Sédécie and Sarrée see Nabuchodonosor come on, Sédécie has time to commend himself to God, and Nabuchodonosor has a monologue of imprecation, before he sees them, and has them dragged to him,

> Mais ne les voy-je pas? les voila mes rebelles,
> Mes traistres, mes mutins, mes sujets infidelles:
> Amenez, attrainez: Hà rustres je vous tiens ...
>
> (1371-73)

In an example later in Act IV, Garnier uses the technique in order to achieve a very different effect. Often, in humanist tragedy, monologues are overheard. Here, however, the Prévot, after his monologue, actually decides to deceive Amital and the queens; and his overheard remarks are therefore loaded. They think he does not know they are there (1591-98). His deception gives them joy. The queens egg on Amital to speak to him, but she will not:

> Abordez-le Madame...Hé la peur me retient (1597)

He continues with the deception for one more line, and then uses the conventional form for perceiving those on stage:

> Ne voy-je pas la Royne? (1599)

which enables the conversation to start.

The irony in this misuse of a convention was only possible if the convention actually meant something. The effect is only really possible in stage terms. Of all the internal evidence for a stage being in the author's mind, this is the most striking example.

The question remains, as to what kind of stage representation was envisaged. The main effect was clearly declamatory. 'Set pieces', whether in the form of large speeches, or formalised discussion, were the order of the day. Above all, the main emphasis was clearly on language and style.

The use of the word 'rhetoric' should help us to understand what was intended; for rhetoric implies the *spoken* word, even if at times, in the late Middle Ages and the Renaissance, it had become confused with poetics. The great set speeches of the ancient orators have their equivalents in this tragedy. One should not forget that, of the five parts of Ciceronian rhetoric, an important one was *pronuntiatio*, or delivery. Nor should one forget that Garnier was a lawyer.

The subtlety of the interplay of themes and references, which could make these plays look as though they were intended for reading, cannot detract from this. The lack of outlets for performance can, admittedly, have meant that authors had readers in mind as well as audiences. But if one discounts the obviously 'reader-orientated' plays such as those of Matthieu, one is left with a manageable erudition, and a store of stock procedures and references, which would be 'visible to the naked eye' of an actual audience, particularly an audience steeped in the classics and the Bible, who would be immediately aware of departures from norms, of side-references to the better-known classics, of variants and mixtures produced from such references, etc. Indeed, even in the most subtle recurrences of themes and images, one must bear in mind that, as well as the intellectual satisfaction available to a reader who perceived them, there was an impact of theme, tone or colour which would affect the hearer, whether he perceived every nuance or not.

Garnier's verse is clearly for speaking. The major effects which he achieves are, to a large extent, based on the dramatic use of rhythm and sound. Important words, important themes, are picked out by rhythmical effects; at the same time, both argument and the expression of emotion depend strongly on a coherent rhythmical line, enriched by the subtle use of sound-colours. One has only to read the major speeches out loud to realise how much is lost by 'silent reading'.

For a genre aimed at the display of language, the greatest exponent is the writer with the greatest linguistic skills. Within the limits of the genre, there is drama; but even that drama is dependent on linguistic effects, and is achieved by linguistic contrasts. What remains in one's mind are the great speeches, the great 'set pieces'. The baker who took part each year in the performances near Angoulême had, as his great piece, 'Pareil aux dieux je marche...'. That speech was one of the most imitated by subsequent writers.

Generations brought up on the certainties of psychological theatre, from the 17th century to the 19th, were of course thrown by this static, poetic theatre. They saw its aims as mere weaknesses, and failed to look for its virtues. Yet the twentieth century is, perhaps, the period that can begin to appreciate this genre anew. The moral certainties that created 'psychological theatre' have been broken down. In the 'theatre of the absurd' we see men as playthings of an absurd fate, helpless to change it; it is their reactions to that fate which interest us. In religious poetic drama, on the other hand, we have returned with Claudel to a fairly static form of theatre, in which the poetic expression of impressionistic feelings and reactions is one of the major effects created by the author. The 'verset claudélien' which dominates his drama from *Tête d'or* to *Le Soulier de satin* is the authentic tone which is remembered by an audience, much as the power of Garnier's verse had been. Add to all this the acceptance of Euripides and Aeschylus as fit dramatists for television-viewing, and one must come to the conclusion that now, more than at any time in the intervening period, French Renaissance tragedy has the possibility of being both understood and appreciated.

2. Les Juifves: the Choice of Biblical Subject

Say on, come to Hecuba
(*Hamlet*, Act II, Sc. 2)

That Garnier should have turned to a Biblical subject for his final and greatest tragedy is not particularly surprising. Amid the neo-classical tragedies of the 16th century some of the most striking had been on Biblical subjects: Buchanan's *Jephthes* and *Baptistes*, Roillet's *Aman*, Rivaudeau's *Aman*, Jean de la Taille's *Saül le furieux* and *La Famine*, not to speak of the Protestant dramas of Bèze and Des Masures.

It was possible, of course, for such tragedies to use the Bible merely as a convenient storehouse of themes on which a suitable neo-classical drama could be based. La Taille's plays, for example, have often been seen in this light. Others, however, while making full use of classical themes and sources, also point a religious moral, often cleverly interleaving it with moral considerations from pagan literature. This *contaminatio* of the religious and the secular can be particularly effective.

Garnier's *Les Juifves* has as its central theme the punishment of the Jews for deserting their God. In his Dedication, the author points out, too, that the play is meant to parallel contemporary truths:

Or vous ay-je icy representé les souspirables calamitez d'un peuple, qui a comme nous abandonné son Dieu. C'est un sujet delectable, et de bonne et saincte edification.

Street has pointed out that this was 'a theme which preoccupied many dramatists at this time, God's punishment of the nation's sin by the scourges of war and other disasters' (*17*, p.22). In the dedications to his secular plays, too, Garnier had described his subjects (civil war in *Cornélie* and *Marc Antoine*, destruction and suffering in *La Troade*) as being a parallel to contemporary events. The difference is that in *Les Juifves* the cause is not in doubt: there is no speculation as to whether it was 'par l'ire du grand Dieu, ou par l'inevitable malignité d'une secrette influence des astres' (Dedication to *La Troade*), but certainty that it is the sin of the Jews that has caused their suffering.

This general moral theme is of the same order as the traditional description of tragedy as having been invented

> pour remonstrer aux roys et grands seigneurs l'incertitude et lubrique instabilité des choses temporelles, a fin qu'ils n'ayent de confiance qu'en la seule vertu.
> (Lazare de Baïf, Dedication to translation of *Hecuba*,
> 6, p.35)

Just as the 'utility' of secular tragedy was to teach kings virtue by showing the instability of fortune, so the 'utility' of religious tragedy was to teach people not to abandon God.

In *Les Juifves* the two themes, religious and secular, are closely intermingled. The condition of Sédécie and of the Jewish people is an 'example' to the audience, in the way that a Renaissance author expected the tragic condition of his main characters to be. 'Que voyla, ma compagne, un beau miroüer pour tous' (586) says the Queen, as she sees Amital and her companions. She is referring, of course, to reversal of Fortune. Sédécie, on the other hand, is aware of his role as an 'example' in religious terms, as well. At his first appearance he declares:

> Peuples qui mesprisez le courroux du grand Dieu [...]
> Helas corrigez-vous, delaissez vostre erreur,
> Que l'exemple de nous vous apporte terreur.
> (1277-82)

These are the two major themes of *Les Juifves*. Most of the subordinate themes in the scenes of discussion are not just used in their own right, but to support them. Though some of these lesser themes have contemporary relevance, there is no trace of any propaganda aim.

Some critics, it is true, have made much of the fact that the figure of Sédécie, and his relationship with Nabuchodonosor, were much used in polemical arguments about the monarchy, during the religious wars. These arguments were based on the reasons given by Ezekiel for God's punishment of Zedekiah:

> Moreover, the word of the Lord came unto me, saying...Behold, the king of Babylon...hath taken of the king's seed, and made a convenant with him, and hath taken an oath of him... But he rebelled against him... Shall he prosper? Shall he escape that doeth such things? or shall he break the covenant, and be delivered? As I live, saith the Lord God, surely in the place where the king dwelleth that made him king, whose oath he despised, and whose covenant he brake, even with him in the midst of Babylon he shall die... Therefore thus saith the Lord God; As I live, surely mine oath that he hath despised, and my covenant that he hath broken, even it will I recompense upon his head. (Ezekiel, XVII, 11-19)

The idea is admittedly an attractive one: God punishes those who break their oaths of loyalty; loyalty is thus owed even to unworthy kings. But there is one problem, as far as this specific play is concerned. Though Sédécie's rebellion is naturally discussed in the play (and mentioned in Garnier's *Dedication*), where it is seen as the immediate cause for Sédécie's punishment by Nabuchodonosor, the reasons given in the play for *God*'s anger with Sédécie and the Jews (produced by the Prophet, the Chorus, and Sédécie himself) all relate to the abandonment of God for false gods. To this is added their crime in not listening to God's prophets. The two major themes are hammered home in the Prophet's first monologue (43-52, 67-86); in Act II's mid-act chorus (311-26, 339-58); in the words of the Chœur des Juifves in Act II (493-96, 533-36); in Sédécie's first speech, in Act IV (1287-94), and in his later statements in this scene (1327-30, 1343-50); and in Sédécie's first speech to Nabuchodonosor (1403-06). (For a full treatment of this question of idolatry in *Les Juifves*, see *20*.)

Sédécie's rebellion, and disloyalty, are of course touched on in the discussions with Nabuchodonosor, who refers to his 'detestable et lasche trahison' (210), his ingratitude (245) and disloyalty (243), his breaking of the alliance (1051), etc. La Royne, too, stresses the seriousness of rebellion, and Nabuchodonosor's justified anger at it. These mentions are, however, all connected with the relationship between Nabuchodonosor and Sédécie; God does not appear to come into it. In passing, there are one or two references to the oath, when Nabuchodonosor refers to Sédécie as 'un Roy parjure, un traistre, un rebelle' (952) and later berates him to his face as 'un ingrat, un infame, un violeur de foy' (1458). But nothing is made of it; these appear to be purely added terms of vituperation. Indeed, Garnier seems merely to be following his source, Josephus, in which 'when he came before him, Nebuchadnezzar began to denounce him as an impious wretch and a violator of treaties' (*Jewish Antiquities*, X, 138-39).

What is interesting is that, despite a strong source in Ezekiel, Garnier's 'religious' characters make no reference to God's wrath at the breaking of the oath; nor (though this is less important) does anyone else. If Garnier had wished to use the Nabuchodonosor-Sédécie relationship to get across a political message, he could hardly have failed to use this source to make the crucial point. Instead, the message which is stressed is a general moral one, as in so many French humanist tragedies.

The Fall of Jerusalem, and the fate of Zedekiah, provide therefore a useful moral subject, with some relationship to the tragic nature of contemporary events. The main aim was nevertheless the creation of a *tragedy*; and it will now be worth our looking at the Biblical subject for its suitability for such treatment, in Renaissance terms.

Why was the specific subject of *Les Juifves* chosen? The fall of Jerusalem provides, of course, a tailor-made subject for a tragedy on the Senecan model. If the subject of tragedy was to contain 'occisions, exils, malheureux definemens de fortunes, d'enfans ou de parents' (*6*, p.52), 'grandes calamitez, meurtres

et adversitez' (*6*, p.35), then the fall of a great city, accompanied
by indiscriminate murders including those of children, by the
prospect of exile for its inhabitants, and by the blinding of the
hero, was an ideal theme. Not only that, but such events had
already been extensively treated by the ancients in relation to the
fall of Troy. Euripides's *The Daughters of Troy* and *Hecuba*,
and Seneca's *Troades*, all deal with this theme; and it is
significant that Garnier had, only four years before *Les Juifves*,
produced his own tragedy of *La Troade* (1579), a portmanteau
affair which gathered together the themes, the scenes and the
speeches from Seneca's and Euripides's treatments of the
subject. In *La Troade* Garnier had appeared more as a co-
ordinator, gathering together for the contemporary audience as
much as possible of what the ancient theatre had written about
the fall of Troy, than as a playwright with a coherent plan of his
own. The imitation was, throughout most of the play, very
close. *Les Juifves* is quite different; it has a tightly-knit plan of
its own, into which such scenes as are imitated from Seneca fit
naturally. The imitation is sparing, and subtly manipulated in
combination with other sources and other themes.

The figure of Hecuba was a powerful one in the Renaissance
consciousness. The fact that, among the very few translations of
the Greek tragedians up to this date, there had been two of
Euripides's *Hecuba* (Latin, by Erasmus, 1506; French, by Baïf
or Bochetel, 1544) speaks for itself, as does the popularity of
Hecuba as a subject for rhetorical *progymnasmata*: 'Qualia
verba dixerit Hecuba post excidium Troianum' ('The kind of
words Hecuba might have said after the fall of Troy') etc. (*25*;
see also *4*, p.109). The 'mobled queen' was a powerful figure.
Hamlet, listening to the First Player's speech depicting the fall
of Troy, interrupts with the impatient words: 'Say on, come to
Hecuba' (Act II, scene 2); and in that portion of his speech the
First Player changes colour, and has tears in his eyes, so that
Hamlet later wonders on the power of his imagination:

> What's Hecuba to him, or he to Hecuba,
> That he should weep for her?

Luckily for Garnier, there *was* a queen-mother in the Biblical story. Garnier, like other Renaissance playwrights, tended not to produce major characters in his tragedies who were not vouched for by history or by another source; and in this case the Bible provided him with Zedekiah's mother, 'Ha-mu-tal, the daughter of Jeremiah of Libnah' (II Kings 24, 18), who, in Josephus, became 'Amital of the city of Lobane' (Josephus, X, 81). She does not, of course, figure in the Biblical description of the fall of Jerusalem. But her existence is enough to enable Garnier to bring her in as a central figure in his tragedy, embodying all the suffering of the defeated people.

The Fall of Jerusalem provided, moreover, an even more important figure for a Renaissance tragedy; the tyrant-figure of Nebuchadnezzar. Tyrant-figures dominate the tragedy of the period; many plays, including religious ones, chose their subjects because of the presence of such a figure. How else can one explain the continuing popularity of Esther-plays, and the fact that so many of them were named not after Esther herself, but after the infamous, tyrannical Haman? (Naogeorgus, *Hamanus*, 1556; Roillet, *Aman*, 1556; Rivaudeau, *Aman*, 1566; Le Devin, *Aman*, ca. 1576; Matthieu, *Aman*, 1589; Montchrestien, *Aman*, 1601).

The historical Nebuchadnezzar, as he is now perceived, would fit the part rather less well than did the sixteenth-century perception of him. Modern archaeological and historical evidence has shown him to have been a man of unusually devout and religious character (in relation to his own gods, of course; but he would have been unlikely to compare himself to the gods, in the impious way Garnier's tyrant does). The Biblical Nebuchadnezzar, on the other hand, measures himself with God, and is brought low because of it (Daniel, 3 and 4). In La Porte's *Epithetes*, that compendium of 16th-century clichés, Nebuchadnezzar's punishment for impiety is given extensive treatment.

Nabuchodonosor roi de Babylone fut en guerre fort heureus, et obtint plusieurs victoires, à cause desquelles on le surnomma le grand; Mais pource qu'il s'orgueillit, et

mesconneut l'auteur d'icelles, il fut par sentence divine
aliéné de son entendement ...   (*30*, p.174 ro.)

The theme of Nebuchadnezzar's animal punishment, which
we shall see as being very important to the patterns of imagery in
this play, was central to Renaissance perceptions of him: 'And
he was driven from men, and did eat grass as oxen' (Daniel IV,
33).

The tyrant-figure also enables, over and above the stock
elements in the model, certain precise borrowings from a further
Senecan play, *Thyestes*. These consist not only of elements in the
three great tyrant speeches in *Les Juifves*, but also form the basis
for the cruel irony practised by both Nabuchodonosor and the
Prévost. They mislead their listeners about their true intentions
in the same way as Atreus misleads Thyestes, when he says, to
the man who has just eaten his own sons:

Be sure that here, in their father's bosom, are thy sons; —
here now, and here shall be; no one of thy children shall be
taken from thee [...] Wholly with his family will I fill the
sire. Thou shalt be satisfied, have no fear of that.
(*Thyestes*, 976-80)

Here again, however, the Biblical source points the author
towards this Senecan irony. Ezekiel had prophesied that
Zedekiah (Sédécie) would never see Babylon; Jeremiah, in
apparent contradiction, had prophesied that he would go into
captivity there, and he in fact did so. Josephus describes his
blinding and captivity as follows:

And thus there befell him what both Jeremiah and Ezekiel
had prophesied to him, namely that he would be captured
and brought to the Babylonian king and speak to him to
his face and with his own eyes look into his eyes, which is
what Jeremiah had said; furthermore, being blinded and
taken to Babylon, he did not see it, as Ezekiel had
foretold... (*29*, X, 141)

Other aspects of the Biblical story which must have attracted for these reasons include the murder of Sédécie's children before his eyes, and his subsequent blinding (which is not only worthy of the classical theatre in its vicious cruelty, but also has a close parallel to Polymestor's fate in Euripides's *Hecuba* and in Garnier's own *La Troade*); and also the figure of Sédécie himself, the man of suffering, the king deserted by Fortune. Sédécie is something more, as Raymond Lebègue has pointed out. As the believer in God suffering at the hands of a pagan tyrant, he also takes his place alongside the Christian martyrs of the mediaeval theatre. His 'Credo' in Act IV is a set piece typical of those pronounced by such figures. In the Biblical story Garnier has thus not only found a character fit for a humanist tragedy; he has also had the added bonus of finding an opportunity to introduce yet another type of 'set piece' as well.

Onto this basic classical frame, Garnier was able to weld further useful Renaissance dramatic features, through his use of the further characters presented to him by the Bible and by history. Sarrée, for example, is a very suitable interlocutor for Sédécie, in that Seraiah the high priest not only is the provider of godly conversation, but also, as the 'quiet prince' described in Jeremiah 51, 59, was someone who had already been a confidant of Sédécie for many years, having accompanied him on a previous visit to Babylon.

Nabuchodonosor's interlocutors, on the other hand, are chosen because of the contrast they present to each other, and the knowledge the audience would already have of them. Amital we have already discussed. Nabuzardan, the captain of the king's guard, was well-known as the man who 'feut entre tous aultres capitaines esleu pour assiéger et ruiner Hierusalem' (*31*, Ch.39). His discussion with Nabuchodonosor is therefore of a different order.

La Royne is perhaps the most important of these characters. The 16th-century audience would presumably have been aware of the existence of that Queen of Babylon, Amuhia the 'Median', on whom Nabuchodonosor lavished his affection by, among other things, erecting a 'hanging garden'. It has also recently been pointed out that it was a common belief, in the

16th century, that the queen who came to Belshazzar after the writing on the wall (Daniel, V, 10-12) and advised him to send for Daniel, was in fact the 'queen-mother' and the wife of Belshazzar's father Nebuchadnezzar (see *19*). These two characteristics thus make of La Royne someone towards whom Nabuchodonosor's attitudes were likely to be different, and also someone whose predictions of reversals of fortune were likely to have great weight for the audience. As we shall see, she has other very important uses as well.

Le Prophète is a complex figure, based in Biblical history, owing much to Jeremiah. Though Jeremiah witnessed the fall of Jerusalem, he remained behind thereafter, and so, historically, could not be depicted as being at Antioch. There are, however, advantages in the general nature of the prophet-figure. He is more impersonal, as the voice and interpreter of God's message; he sums up the characteristics of a number of the prophets; and he is mysterious. This is one of Garnier's most important figures in the play; his role will be discussed more fully later.

3. Arias, Recitatives and Choruses

> We'll have a speech straight. Come,
> give us a taste of your quality; come, a
> passionate speech ... I heard thee
> speak me a speech once, but it was
> never acted; or, if it was, not above
> once; for the play, I remember,
> pleased not the million ... One speech
> in it I chiefly loved ...
>
> (*Hamlet*, Act II, Sc.2).

A humanist tragedy was, as we have seen, built up on the basis of a series of 'set pieces', stylised forms which served not only as a framework for the author's display of style and language, but also as a basis for an interplay of ideas, images and themes.

Les Juifves is remarkable not because it is entirely made up of set pieces like any other humanist tragedy, but because of the coherence of the effects obtained by the plan within which they are set. The chart on pp.30-31 gives a skeleton plan of the pattern involved.

With very few exceptions, the major speeches and discussions in the play fall clearly into the various stock categories, or are based upon scenes in well-known sources. The main departure from custom lies in the final scene of Act V, which is all the more striking for this reason.

The pieces of the jigsaw are fitted together in such a way as to create a cumulative effect, and at the same time to create oppositions and contrasts. The sombre, gloom-laden opening monologue of the Prophète in Act I is succeeded by the proud, boastful tyrant speech of Nabuchodonosor at the beginning of Act II; Biblical imagery gives way to pagan. Acts II and III are dominated by the question of Sédécie's fate, and of Nabuchodonosor's power. These essentially static acts prepare the ground for the issues and themes of Acts IV and V. Within

ACT IV	1277-1300	Sédécie	Monologue of penitence
	1301-1352	Sédécie-Sarrée	Discussion on fortune, etc.
	1353-1362	Sédécie	Prayer
	1363-1390	Nabuchodonosor	Tyrant monologue, followed by speech railing against Sédécie
	1391-1418	Sédécie	Declaration of faith (martyr speech)
	1419-1478	Nabuchodonosor-Sédécie	Argument on punishment
	1479-1489	Sédécie	Vituperatio
	1490-1500	Nabuchodonosor-Sédécie	Exchange of insults
	1501-1504	Nabuchodonosor	[Short comment]
	1505-1564	Chœur	Chorus
	1565-1730	Prévost, Amital, Roynes	Scene loosely based on *Troades*
	1731-1752	Amital	Farewell to children, and declaration of faith
	1753-1764	Roynes	Lamentation
	1765-1836	Chœur	Chorus
ACT V	1837-1870	Prophète	Grand Monologue
	1871-2002	Prophète, Amital, Roynes	Récit and framework
	2003-2076	Amital-Roynes	Lamentation
	2077-2092	Prophète	[Transition]
	2093-2130	Sédécie, Prophète	[Grand scene]
	2131-2172	Prophète	Prophecy

them, opportunities are given not only for lamentations, that mainstay of Renaissance tragedy, but also for enumeration of past misfortunes, and a magnificent *récit* of the Fall of Jerusalem.

With Act IV, and the first appearance of Sédécie, we return to a fully religious tone, in his monologue of penitence, his prayer, and his declaration of faith. Nabuchodonosor is placed in contrast with him, in one of the most remarkable scenes in the play. The rest of Acts IV and V is based on the carrying-out of the designs that have been discussed in the previous two acts. They contain the scene of the children being taken away from their mothers, the *récit* of the fate of Sédécie and the children, the lamentations of the queens, the entry of the blinded Sédécie, and the Prophet's commentary upon the events, which brings the play to a powerful ending, full of Biblical tone, with the prophecy of the fall of Babylon and the coming of Christ.

It would be wrong to think of this pattern of set pieces as being in any way restrictive. The effects achieved by it can be 'dramatic' in a completely different sense from our modern conception of the term. It will be useful at this point to examine some of the forms which are used.

The expository monologue — The Prophet

Of the various forms of exposition practised by the ancients, and by Renaissance dramatists, by far the most popular was the monologue. This could be pronounced either by one of the characters in the play or, more commonly, by somebody outside the action, often a supernatural conveyor of the decisions of fate or the gods, such as a god or a ghost. Two purposes were served, in classical tragedy: the purveying of information and the creation of an atmosphere. In the Renaissance period, the first of these became of less importance, because the authors, relying on the erudition of their audience, presumed them to know the story already. What was retained was the creation of a suitable mood, often together with a statement of the reasons for the wrath of the gods.

Garnier's first four plays had all opened with a monologue. Of these, two (*Porcie* and *Hippolyte*) had been spoken by a supernatural being, a Fury and the Ghost of Aegeus, who both succeeded in creating an atmosphere of death and hellish foreboding. His next two plays, however, *La Troade* and *Antigone*, had seen a change of custom; the former opened with a scene shared by Hecuba and the chorus, the second with a dialogue between Edipe and Antigone. This is explained, however, by the fact that in each case he was closely following the opening scenes of Seneca's plays upon the same subjects (*Troades*, 1-62; *Phoenissae*, 1-319).

As the theme of *Les Juifves* was so similar to that of *La Troade*, and as Renaissance audiences gave so much importance to the theme of Hecuba, one might well have expected Garnier to open *Les Juifves* with an emotive scene between Amital and the Chorus, as in *La Troade*. Instead, while keeping such a scene for later in the play, he opens with a monologue by Le Prophète.

This could, of course, be seen merely as a return to his former custom. There is more to it than that, however. This tragedy, while remaining so classical in form, is highly Biblical in mood, in atmosphere, in language. This is particularly true of Acts I and V. Amital and her chorus, in their lamentations, do achieve an effective mingling of classical and Biblical imagery; but the effect is nevertheless too reminiscent of the classical sources. To give a powerful Biblical tone to his whole tragedy, Garnier needed an opening monologue which, while being in the classical mode, nevertheless owed nothing, as far as language and imagery were concerned, to sources other than the Bible. This monologue would give God's message, the reason for the events of the play.

But who should give God's message? God Himself? Impossible, in the sixteenth century, even though He had appeared in mediaeval plays. An angel? Flat, and too much like the effects of the mediaeval theatre. A mere mortal? Surely not.

His eventual solution achieves the apparently impossible. It mingles the heavenly and the earthly in a figure which speaks with the powerful tones of supernatural doom, and yet is human enough to reappear within the play itself, to underline the message once more in the concluding scenes.

The tone, that of the Biblical prophets, underlines the inevitability of fate as effectively as its classical counterpart. The first six lines of the play establish this tone, from the repeated 'Jusques à quand ... jusqu'à quand ...', reminiscent of the Psalms, through the reference to the forty years in the wilderness, to the stock Biblical image for God's punishment, 'the hand of God'. Throughout the speech, onto major sources such as Exodus, the Psalms, etc., are grafted further colourful Biblical images of a stock kind, which would be well-known to Garnier's public; as opposed to producing striking or original effects, imagery here performs a peculiarly Renaissance task, that of conjuring up a familiar atmosphere and tone through the use of stock images.

The speech as a whole is typical of Garnier's techniques in this play. The tone and content are Biblical, but the form is a brilliant example of Renaissance rhetoric. It is ordered in form, and highly charged effects are achieved by the use of rhetorical figures, the most obvious of which is the use of repetition.

The speech is divided into two main sections: an invocation to God (1-42), and an address to the people of Jerusalem itself (43-90). The first section progresses, at first, in an orderly manner from one theme to another, in reasonably equal sections: How long, O Lord? (1-6); forgive us (7-12); remember your promise (13-17); if we do not worship you, who will? (18-22), ending with two lines (23-24) summing up with a plea for pity.

The past is then evoked, but in a way typical of spoken rhetoric. The theme — that all God's past benefits will have been in vain if He deserts his people now — is plugged home (25-38) by the insistent repetition of phrases meaning 'in vain'. Where a lesser writer might have monotonously reproduced the same phrase, Garnier achieves a strong effect through variation: 'Vainement ... vainement ... Pourneant ... en vain ... en vain ...

pourneant'. This enumeration gives a sense of tension and expectancy; we are waiting to see how the sentence, and the tension, will be resolved. And they are of course, by the satisfying four lines starting 'Si ores ...' (39-42).

Turning to the people, the Prophet now blames them for ignoring his words (43-51) and describes the result of this (52-60); note, again, the balance. The description of the rape of the city is particularly effective, not only because of the violent imagery, but also because of the rhetorical device whereby the speaker breaks off to relate the effect of the memory of it on him (59-60). For six lines (61-66), the Prophet now addresses the city itself, bewailing its fate, before he comes to the reasons for its downfall, the turning to false gods (67-84).

This section is based closely on Jeremiah (67-76), and on Psalm 115 (77-84). It then moves insensibly, in mid-sentence, into an evocation of God ('Au lieu de l'Eternel ...' 84-86), and the speech ends with a plea to the people to turn back to Him. The logical sequence of the speech is thus satisfyingly rounded off, bringing the people, and God (both of whom have been told to turn to each other) together. The effect is heightened, in a way typical of Garnier, by a break in the rhythm followed by a return to balance. The emotional cry of the Prophet, consisting of a breathless, urgent repetition followed by a broken sequence of single verbs separated by commas: 'Amande amande toy, jeusne, pleure, souspire' is resolved by the calmer, more regular rhythm: 'A fin que de ton dos ses glaives il retire'.

The choice of the Prophet to introduce the play enabled this relationship of classical form and Biblical tone and imagery to be established from the start of the play. The right mood of foreboding has been achieved, and the theme of punishment has been effectively introduced. It is now taken up by the Chorus, which moves from the question as to why God is angry with their misdeeds, to the whole question of the Fall of Man.

The tyrant speech

In the stock Renaissance figure of the tyrant, no nuances at all were to be expected. A tyrant was, in the words of La Porte, 'maupiteus, cruel, usurpateur, fier, meschant, execrable, inhumain, ambitieus, mauvais, inique, oppresseur, superbe' etc. (*30*, p.170 vo). Once Nabuchodonosor came on the stage and launched into his first tyrant speech, the audience would have realised (if they had not known so already) that there was no hope for Sédécie.

Nabuchodonosor is in this sense a typical tyrant; but, in this play where man's relationship to God is to be one of the central themes, his impiety is perhaps his most important feature (and, as we have seen, probably one of the reasons for the choice of this subject); as such, it needs to be stressed from the start. The traditional 'tyrant speech' contained this element as one among several; the author's aim therefore had to be to place it in greater prominence.

The tyrant speech took its origins partly from Seneca (and in particular from a speech by Atreus in that playwright's *Thyestes* (line 885 onwards), partly from the 'boasts' of pagan tyrants in mediaeval literature; but the form had taken off on its own wings, and what had originally been individual examples of dramatic expression became, in the Renaissance, part of a formalised and predictable pattern. Fixed points in that pattern were:

1. A periphrasis (often lengthy) for 'in the whole world'.

2. A statement of the fact that in the whole world *either* everyone fears your name, *or* that nobody is equal to you, *or* that nobody is so favoured by the gods.

3. A comparison between oneself and the gods, in hybristic form.

4. Occasionally, a parallel between the gods' rule of heaven, and the tyrant's of earth. (This particular characteristic, borrowed from 'pagan' speeches in mediaeval literature, lent itself to some superb parodies, such as Satan's speech in Bèze's *Abraham sacrifiant*: 'Dieu regne en haut: et bien, je regne en bas'.)

5. Often, the mention of someone (usually a conquered enemy) who can witness to the tyrant's greatness.

All this, often at great length, was far from the simple speech by Seneca's Atreus; indeed, I have not found an example, until *Les Juifves*, of a tyrant speech which uses the actual opening words (or an approximation to them) of the Senecan speech. This is what Garnier does here, with a striking transformation of Seneca's 'Aequalis astris gradior' ('I walk, equal to the stars') into 'Pareil aux Dieux je marche'. The transition from Prophet (Act I) to pagan king (Act II), from God to the gods, is thus startlingly presented to the audience. Moreover, unlike other tyrant speeches, this one launches straight into a hybristic statement, unhampered by detail.

Typically, however, the speech thereafter leaves Seneca, and returns to the Renaissance pattern. Of Atreus's speech only the first phrase has been taken by Garnier. The Renaissance pattern is followed, but it is 'speeded up' and simplified, to match the trenchant opening. Thus the 'place' periphrasis, which in a writer like Muret (*Caesar*, Act I) had taken six lines, and which had been similarly elaborate in the tyrant speech in Garnier's own *Marc Antoine*:

> Soit où Phébus attelle au matin ses chevaux,
> Où la nuict les reçoit, recreus de leurs travaux,
> Où les flammes du ciel bruslent les Garamantes,
> Où souffle l'Aquilon ses froidures poignantes ...
>
> (*Marc Antoine*, Act IV)

becomes the simple: 'et depuis le reveil/Du Soleil blondissant jusques à son sommeil'.

The declaration that he is *nonpareil* is similarly short and striking: 'Nul ne se parangonne à ma grandeur Royale'. It is followed by an equally terse statement of the traditional hybristic theme: 'En puissance et en biens Jupiter seul m'egale'. The first four lines have punched the audience, which would have been used to rather more leisurely tyrant speeches, right between the eyes. They are, thereafter, given a very much lengthier treatment of what, when it occurred in other tyrant speeches, had been a rather less important feature: the parallels between the gods' rule of heaven, and the tyrant's of earth. In this way the importance, in this play, of Nabuchodonosor's

impiety, is stressed from the start. Finally, Nabuchodonosor
turns to a 'witness' of his greatness, 'cet Hebrieu', Sédécie. This,
in turn, leads into the stock discussion of clemency or rigour
from victor to vanquished.

The imbalance as compared with the known structure of the
tyrant speech points out to the aware audience the importance of
the theme which has been singled out for fuller treatment. What
one should not forget in all this, however, is that the power of
Garnier's verse in itself made this the most effective tyrant
speech in French Renaissance tragedy, a speech which was to be
quoted, recited, copied, plagiarised and admired for decades to
come.

'Contaminatio' — The lamentations of Amital and Les Roynes

Lamentations were the essence of humanist tragedy.
Imitation, too, was important; so when a suitable source was
available one used it. The lamentations of Hecuba and her
women in Seneca's *Troades* formed a perfect set piece for
imitation. It is hardly surprising that Garnier should have turned
to it.

The parallel is clearly drawn, from Amital's first appearance.
The tone and content of her first speech (367-92) owe a great
deal to Hecuba's final speech in *Troades* (lines 1170-76), where
she calls for death, and asks why it shuns her. As with the
Prophet and Nabuchodonosor, Garnier establishes the role of
his character powerfully in the first few lines of her first tirade.
The phrase 'Je suis le malheur mesme' sums up in five words the
Hecuba-figure of Renaissance tragedy.

Amital is, however, more than that. She is the mother of the
Jewish king, and the city that has fallen is Jerusalem. Above all,
she and her women are the sole voices, in Acts II and III, to
convey that Biblical tone which has been so effectively set by the
Prophet. Amid the pagan atmosphere, these voices must be
heard.

So it is that the mingling of classical and Biblical sources
becomes paramount in their set pieces. Where the major source
is Seneca, as in Amital's opening speech, we nevertheless find

references to 'Dieu du Ciel, Dieu d'Aron'; where the major
source is Biblical, as in the enumeration of past misfortunes
(397-448), we nevertheless find a deathbed description (403-16)
typical of secular Renaissance tragedy, which owes some of its
detail to Seneca's *Hercules Oetaeus*, a play which Garnier had
already used extensively for his *Marc-Antoine*.

It is in the lamentations which follow (449-536), however, that
the most striking example of *contaminatio* of the two areas of
source-material takes place. These lamentations form a striking
tableau; they also form a perfect combination between the
lamentations of Hecuba and her women from *Troades*, and the
Biblical lamentations from the Psalms and from Jeremiah.

Amital's initial exhortation to the women to weep (459-70) is
an elaboration on Seneca's *Troades* (lines 63-65). Garnier had
already elaborated on this passage in his own *La Troade*
(117-24), and the repetitions of 'Pleurons' (with Jerusalem
replacing Ilion), and the initial rhyme of 'captives...rives...', are
merely some of the details which show that Garnier is here
plundering his own previous artistic locker:

> Mais pourquoy, cher troupeau: pourquoy, filles captives,
> N'emplissez-vous de cris ces resonnantes rives?
> Pourquoy cessent vos pleurs, et pourquoy cessez-vous
> D'ouvrir vostre poitrine et la plomber de coups?
> Pleurons nostre Ilion, ô filles, pleurons Troye,
> El que le Ciel sanglant nos cris funebres oye.
>
> (La Troade, 117-22)

The use of the word 'rives' (which has no equivalent in the
Senecan original) nevertheless turns our thoughts in another
direction. We remember the imagery of the Psalms: 'By the
waters of Babylon, there we sat down and wept' (Psalm 137, v.1.
This psalm is imitated more fully in the Chorus at the end of Act
III). The effect is underlined by the Jewish women's reference
(472) to lamenting 'malheurs Hebraïques' by this 'bord' in
'tristes cantiques' (i.e. psalms).

Amital returns to Seneca (*Troades*, 84-98) in her exhortations
(474-76) to display the outward signs of grief: baring their

breasts, raining blows upon themselves with their hands, tearing their hair. But here again, as Lebègue has pointed out, a Biblical note is added in the form of the reference to sackcloth and ashes. Ashes are indeed mentioned by Seneca (*Troades*, 101-02), but the combination of sackcloth with them is a purely Biblical notion (see Esther IV, i, Jonah III, 5-6, etc.).

The dialogued Chorus of lamentation which follows (447-536) is highly Biblical in tone, and indeed part of it is based upon the Lamentations of Jeremiah (lines 481-84, for example, are reminiscent of Lamentations II, 8 and I, 8). Further Biblical references abound in the imagery, moreover. However, typically, Amital turns, in lines 509-24, to more classical turns of phrase (e.g. line 509, 'O trois fois malheureuse nuit') and a passage loosely based on *Troades*, which reminds us of her Hecuba role.

It is important to note the last few lines of this lyrical lamentation (533-36). Here the Chœur des Juifves, departing from sources, makes a plea for Sédécie to turn from idolatry, and live in God's law. The theme is taken up in Amital's prayer which follows, with her reference to Manasseh, who was saved from Babylon, and returned to God.

This prayer (541-64) is, in form, a magnificent example of a classical speech of supplication ('O seigneur ... qui ... qui ... qui ... pren de nous compassion'). The detail which fills it out is strongly Biblical, as God's past benefits are listed. It is enhanced by Garnier's exquisite sense of the rhythmical and repetitive nature of desperate supplication:

> Pren Seigneur, pren Seigneur, de nous compassion,
> Aye, Seigneur, pitié de la pauvre Sion.
>
> (557-58)

Like the formal lamentations, it ends with a strong reference to idolatry. This almost artificial addition (563-64) to the form of the prayer is yet another way of singling out the theme.

Contaminatio is used, in these lamentations, to provide the Biblical presence in Act II, and yet to use the most well-known classical source for lamentation by a group of women on the fall

of a city. The skilful use of this technique provides overtones of
a particularly rich kind.

Stichomythia

The scenes of discussion are a fascinating area for study, and
will receive it (see pp.59-67). Much of their fascination lies in the
field of ideas. There is one respect, however, in which certain
parts of those discussions have a strong formal interest, and that
is in the passages of stichomythia.

Strictly speaking, stichomythia is a dialogue in which the
replies are of a regular length; one can have half-line, one-line or
two-line examples of the form. Regularity is the essence of it,
though there *is* such a thing as irregular stichomythia, which
transfers, for example, from one-line to half-line regularity, and
back. There *must*, however, be a general tendency to regularity,
otherwise it is merely dramatic conversation.

Where the Greeks had often used this form for question-and-
answer sessions, conveying information, in Seneca it was most
often used for close-knit dispute. This became extremely
popular in the Renaissance. Plays became filled with long
disputes in very strict form, in which arguments were taken up
and turned around, often with parallel expression and merely
one or two words changed in each exchange.

It could be extremely effective. The quick-fire exchanges
could vary the tempo of a scene, contrasting strongly with the
long tirades. The audience could enjoy the cut-and-thrust of
argument, the verbal dexterity of the author, the variation
within a strict form.

Occasionally, of course, it got over-used, particularly by some
of Garnier's successors. But in itself it was an essential part of
the enjoyment of the contemporary audience. Garnier had
always used a certain amount of it in his plays; but it is
interesting to note that, unlike many of his contemporaries, he
had a predilection for irregular stichomythia, interspersing for
example half-lines and one-and-a-half-lines within the regular
pattern.

Considering the number of scenes of discussion in *Les Juifves*, stichomythia is used comparatively sparingly. Indeed, in the discussion between Nabuchodonosor and Amital it does not figure at all. This is presumably because in that scene we are not dealing with the cold examination of pros and cons, but with the various emotional arguments which Amital successively puts to the tyrant.

It is typical of Garnier that stichomythia should often be used not merely for its own sake, but to make some subtle or effective point, either by its placing or its form. This is not necessarily true, of course, of all examples. The stichomythia in the Nabuchodonosor-Nabuzardan scene is aesthetically satisfying, and rounds off the scene in a regular and rounded manner; but there is little else to say about it.

In the scene between Nabuchodonosor and La Royne, however, the initial stichomythia (903-28) has a precise purpose. It is on the stock clemency-rigour theme, and lulls us into a sense of *déjà vu*; the parallel but contradictory statements remain verbally and syntactically very close to each other. But Garnier is preparing some surprises for us, which this formality and stylisation will bring out even more forcibly. The argument gradually moves from clemency and rigour to the duties of a prince in this respect; the return of the theme of the tyrant, who can do what he likes, and who owes it to his greatness to be feared, is countered by the Queen with statements about the prince's duty of moderation. It is then that the pattern, and the argument, decisively break down, and the major theme of the dialogue emerges. The Queen suggests that he should be like God, whose power is supreme, but who is moderate.

The mention of God pushes Nabuchodonosor into a violent statement which contains the full flourish of his initial tyrant speech: 'Dieu fait ce qu'il luy plaist, et moy je fay de mesme' (928). This abruptly brings the stichomythia to an end. The Queen reacts with horror. The calm, almost impersonal argument is abandoned, and in a lengthy speech she begs him to speak in a more wholesome manner, warns him of God's punishment of *hybris*, and introduces the central concerns of this discussion.

In the scene between Nabuchodonosor and Sédécie the stichomythia (1421-56) represents the reasonably calm discussion on 'quality' and punishment out of which is to come the violent exchange of insults in the later part of the scene. As such it provides, formally, the calm ordered basis for the arguments. It is fascinating to note, however, that at the height of the later furious argument there is a short exchange of two single lines (too short to be stichomythia) which nevertheless turns one of the techniques of stichomythia to another purpose. It repeats a phrase from the one line to the other, but not to counter a reasoned argument; it uses the technique to pile up abuse in a wild and almost childish manner:

NABUCHODONOSOR
Tu sembles un mâtin, qui abaye et qui grongne
SÉDÉCIE
C'est toy-mesmes mâtin, qui te pais de charongne.

It is not merely by the 'placing' of stichomythia that Garnier achieves his effects, however. Given the great formality of the technique he is, as with other 'set pieces', able to achieve great effects by even the most minor adjustments within the set piece itself.

A good example of this is to be found in the scene between Amital and La Royne. Amital is asking the Queen to intercede on Sédécie's behalf. Their conversation has started with a discussion of fortune, and the related themes of 'quality' and kingship; now the tempo is quickened into a formal passage of stichomythia (645) in which Amital calls for the punishment to fit the crime, and the Queen talks about the rights of a victorious king. Amid these stock arguments a most interesting formal variant occurs; it occurs because of a clash between two different techniques of argument, both of which would be very familiar to the spectator: (1) quick-fire stichomythia, which relies for its effect upon formal balance, and on concision; (2) the custom, in more leisurely scenes of argument, of using extended similes, often from the realm of nature.

Amital clearly decides to use such an image; and she picks one of the most well-used ones available. In debates on clemency, the lion was often used as an example of magnanimity towards a weak opponent. This image stems back to classical times (e.g. Ovid, *Tristia* III), and also figures in mediaeval texts. Garnier had already produced it in his earlier play *Porcie*, where Marc-Antoine uses it to great effect:

> Semblable au preux lion, au lion généreux,
> Qui ne daigne lever sa grande patte croche
> Qu'encontre un fier taureau, qui bien cornu s'approche,
> Furieux combatant, et veut plustost mourir
> Que devant sa genice une honte encourir.
> Là, fumant de courroux, ce grand guerrier se rue
> Au col de l'ennemy voué pour la charrue,
> Qu'il tirasse et secoue avecques tel effort,
> Qu'encore qu'il se monstre et belliqueux et fort,
> Qu'il roidisse ses nerfs, que de pieds et de teste
> Il choque renfrongné la forestière beste
> Sur l'estomach crineux, et que du coup doublé,
> Le lion plein d'ardeur en demeure troublé,
> Il l'atterre pourtant et demy hors d'haleine
> Fait couler de sa gorge une rouge fonteine.
> Lors retournant vaincueur en son roc cavernier,
> S'il trouve à l'impourveu quelque chien moutonnier,
> Qui tremblant et criant plat à ses pieds se couche,
> Il passe plus avant et piteux ne luy touche.
>
> (*Porcie*, 1242-60)

Such a leisurely approach is, however, impossible in stichomythia, however effective (in sixteenth century terms) it is in other contexts. The audience's surprise is great, therefore, when it looks as though Amital is about to launch out into just such an extended image. She is, however, immediately interrupted by the Queen:

> AMITAL
> Le genereux Lion.
> LA ROYNE
> J'entends bien: mais le crime est de rebellion.
>
> (653-54)

The technique is unusual, to say the least. It relies upon the audience's knowledge of the clichés of dramatic language. In three short words a whole lengthy image is summed up, and put into the balance of the argument. Moreover, the audience is given the aesthetic satisfaction of hearing the pattern of stichomythia, which had looked as though it was going to be fundamentally disturbed, continuing perfectly. It is perhaps not too fanciful to conjecture that Garnier is here teasing his audience, appearing to offer one thing and then giving another.

It is also a significant pointer (as in the Nabuchodonosor-Royne scene) to what is going to be the serious import of the scene. The stock arguments are marshalled into line in formal stichomythia; that pattern is then broken, not by a 'genereux Lion' digression, but a dramatic short-line statement ('Il vous feroit mourir'), in response to which, Amital breaks out in a twelve-line speech. This, by breaking the quick-fire argument pattern, stresses the importance of the theme of death. The idea could have been put across in the one line (662) which opens the speech; but, as we shall see, the 'death' theme is of great importance in the pattern of ideas which link the various clemency-rigour discussions.

As though to underline this, the succeeding discussion reverts to very strict single-line stichomythia of an even more stylised kind, with parallel phrases matching each other almost word for word. This exchange (679-86) is on the stock theme of the suicide debate found in many Renaissance tragedies. By its very formality it makes Amital's speech stand out in even greater relief. It is succeeded, of course, by the framework for Amital's great *récit*.

Tonal contrasts between set pieces

The most obvious example of this is La Royne's *aubade* in Act II (566-78). Up to this point, the tone of the play has been one of unrelieved gloom. The Prophet's invocation of God's wrath, and his call to repentance; Nabuchodonosor's revelation of cruelty, pride and viciousness; the lamentations of Amital and the Jewish women; these are the stuff of which humanist tragedy is made. Garnier had nevertheless already shown, in his *Hippolyte*, the value of a contrast in tone. There, in Act I, immediately after the dark, hellish tone of the introductory monologue by the Ghost of Aegeus, with its foretelling of the full scale of the tragedy to come, Hippolyte had come on, and invoked the beauty of the dawn. The dark colours turned to light:

> Jà l'Aurore se leve, et Phebus, qui la suit,
> Vermeil fait recacher les flambeaux de la nuict.
> Jà ses beaux limonniers commencent à respandre
> Le jour aux animaux, qui ne font que l'attendre.
> Jà les monts sourcilleux commencent à jaunir
> Sous le char de ce dieu qu'ils regardent venir.
> O beau soleil luisant, belle et claire planette ...
>
> (*Hippolyte*, 143-49)

The tone soon changes back to gloom, with the depiction of Hippolyte's terrible dream; but the impact of the change of tone remains.

It is fascinating that, for the similar change of tone in *Les Juifves*, Garnier should again have chosen the form of the *aubade*, the invocation to dawn. Here it follows directly on the lamentations of the Jewish women.

Garnier even opens with a phrase already used in the Hippolyte *aubade*: 'O beau Soleil luisant ...'. The *aubade* continues by linking the happy aspects of dawn with the joy of the conquerors, for whom the rising sun reveals 'le desirable fruit/Du sort victorieux'. The mood is, of course, shattered when she becomes aware of the lamenting women, and immediately feels pity for them.

The other great example of a contrasting tone of this kind is Amital's speech of joy at the end of Act III (1203-12). This has, of course, been produced by Nabuchodonosor's ironical and misleading promises, and has no basis in reality. Nevertheless, we get a rapid shaft of light in the gathering gloom. The tone is Biblical, 'Sus touchons le tabour, sus la flûte entonnons,/ Prenons harpe et guiterre ...' with strong reminiscences of individual psalms. It not only contrasts with the tone of the rest of the act; it also parallels Amital's instructions to the Jewish women in Act II: 'Rompons nos vestemens' etc. (473). Here, as there, she is calling for actions to express emotions: tearing of hair, sackcloth and ashes, for despair; playing of instruments for joy.

The choice of this theme is not accidental; it enables the Chorus, which is unconvinced, to reject the idea in the words of Psalm 137, which had also been used in their lamentations in Act II. This time, they ask *how they can sing and play instruments*, and insist that if they ever forget Zion

> Nostre langue tienne au gosier,
> Et nostre dextre
> Pour les instruments manier
> Ne soit adextre:

'We hanged our harps upon the willows ... and they that wasted us required of us mirth, saying, Sing us one of the songs of Zion. How shall we sing the Lord's song in a strange land? If I forget thee, O Jerusalem, let my right hand forget her cunning. If I do not remember thee, let my tongue cleave to the roof of my mouth ...' (Psalm 137, 2-9). The use of all but the first verse of this psalm as a source reminds the audience of that very first verse, 'By the waters of Babylon, there we sat down, yea, we wept ...', which permeated the women's lamentations in Act II (see p.39). Amital's speech of joy is therefore not only seen as contrary to the dominant tone; it, and Nabuchodonosor's irony, have provided the springboard for a close textual allusion which links the lamentations within the two acts.

The chorus's rejection of her joy is not, of course, caused by rejection of her belief in the tyrant's words, but by the sorrows of exile, which even the news of their children's safety cannot allay. Its introduction at this point is, however, particularly effective, as the dominant mood is brought back, in a verse-form which accentuates their mournful resignation by its alternation of long and short lines, the latter producing a kind of 'dying fall'.

The récits, *and their framework*

Of all the set pieces, the *récit* is the one which can contain the greatest variety of poetic techniques: narrative, description, extended similes, and at times reported speech. Most of its techniques are correspondingly different from those of the *tirades*.

The format is, of course, artificial. News of great importance, which should be given succinctly, is elaborated on at great length. Admittedly, in the Greeks the messenger speech had usually been a straightforward narrative, conveying a clear message to the listener, in which the few decorative elements were subsidiary to the theme. Seneca, however, had developed the form in a completely different way. The form, which had been free and easy, became stylised; similes and descriptions became an excuse for long digressions. The whole thing became far more static and ornamental, an opportunity for linguistic and rhetorical display.

The two great *récits* in *Les Juifves* are both masterpieces of the genre. In them, Garnier uses the stock stylised techniques but, through the immediacy of his verse, creates a vivid and at times exciting picture.

Amital's description of the Fall of Jerusalem, and the capture of Sédécie (697-798), shows us some of his techniques. It starts with the usual formal setting of the scene, either in space or time. Unlike some of the excessive examples in Seneca and other Renaissance tragedians, however (the setting of the scene for the death of Astyanax, in Seneca's *Troades*, takes twenty lines), this is a short four-line evocation of time (697-700). Not only that; it is also of structural importance to the *récit* itself, in that it stresses the length of time that the beleaguered city has been without food. As this topic is treated, the very rhythm of the verse gives the impression of the lack of energy produced by hunger. Some crisp lines (703-08) have given the history of the siege up to this time; but now 'La faim, plus que le fer, palles nous combatoit', and the people are without vigour:

> Le peuple allangouré, sans courage, sans force,
> Descharné se trainoit, n'ayant rient que l'escorce

Qui luy couvroit les os, et ceste maigre faim
Estouffoit les enfants en demandant du pain

(711-14)

After a short interruption in the *récit*, and a few general remarks
by Amital, however, the tempo quickens with the Babylonian
attack. Again, a time description is introduced (735-40); but it is
to stress the silence and peace of the night. The silence is broken
by the attack, suddenly, as the Babylonians scale the walls with
'grands hurlemens' (742). The speed and decision of their
actions is stressed by the succession of active verbs in parallel:

... *échele* les rempars,
Donne dedans la breche, et ne trouvant defense,
Rangé par escadrons dans la ville *s'élance*:
Gaigne les carrefours, *s'empare* des lieux forts ...

(742-45)

As the population is put to the sword, the tempo quickens, and
the indiscriminate and chaotic nature of what is going on 'pesle-
mesle' is stressed not only by the breathless succession of
individual words separated by commas, but also, in line 751, by
the use of *vers rapportés*, a device from lyric poetry in which
parallel subjects and verbs are separated, but placed in the same
order.

Les femmes, les enfans, et les hommes âgez
Tombent sans nul esgard pesle-mesle esgorgez.
Le sang, le feu, le fer, coule, flambe, resonne

(749-51)

The chaos is filled with the noise of trumpets and drums, yet
(and the chiasmus adds to this impression) where they are, and
how many, is as unclear as the scene: 'On entend maint tabour,
mainte trompette sonne' (753). The dead are everywhere, and
the enemy's carnage is indiscriminate.

In contrast to this violent scene, the king's flight takes on a
tone of anguished secrecy. As in the Biblical story (II Kings 25,

Jeremiah 39) they flee by 'une poterne', 'en segret'. The wild path by which they flee is described in ten vivid lines (761-70); again, a description is there not merely for its own sake, but to evoke a contrast. The light of the fires of the destroyed city now turns to darkness. The small band, fleeing 'en frayeur' by 'voyes secrettes', is surrounded by a starless night: 'La nuit estoit obscure, et nos humides yeux/Ne voyoyent pour conduite aucune lampe aux cieux' (773-74). Garnier's use of the sense of sight has been particularly effective in this, as in many other of his *récits*; but now, the immediacy of the scene is brought home by the use of another sense. As dawn breaks 'Nous entendons hennir/Des chevaux'. This first hint of the pursuit is swiftly followed by the sight of the pursuers '... et soudain nous les voyons venir'. The action suddenly speeds up again, as the Jews run around in chaos and fear, 'deça delà courir'. The king alone remains motionless, 'trop attendry de cœur'.

The sharp, quickly-depicted scene of the capture gives, in contrast to the chaos of the vanquished, a picture of a series of decisive actions, with once again a series of active verbs produced in parallel:

> Aussi tost les coureurs nous viennent *enfermer*,
> *Se saisissent* de nous, *font* le Roy desarmer,
> Nous *ameinent* icy, hommes, femmes ensemble.
>
> (793-95)

The whole *récit* has been a drama in miniature, with contrasting scenes of calmness and action, of light and dark, of noise and silence; the outcome of that drama is short and decisive.

The *dénouement récit* in Act V is a masterpiece of its particular genre. Such *récits* had a fairly fixed form; a setting in time or place would be followed by a narrative in which various types of fairly lengthy digression would be exploited. These would include long Homeric similes, as in ancient epic; long descriptions of places, people or animals; long passages in direct speech; and often, for further effect, a depiction of the impression made by the scene on the spectators.

In many humanist tragedies, indeed in many of Garnier's,

these techniques were used to the full. After all, the very concept of a long speech to tell simple facts was unreal in itself; why, even when a messenger was asked 'raconte briesvement' (*Porcie*, 1435), should not the form be filled out as much as possible? Thus, in *Cornélie*, the messenger speech contains a speech of 32 lines by Pompey before going into battle; in *Hippolyte*, Thésée interrupts the narrative, at the appearance of the monster, to ask 'Quelle figure avoit ce monstre si énorme?', whereupon he is treated to 13 lines of minute description, before the messenger continues to describe what happened to Hippolyte; and, at the crucial moment, as Hippolyte's horses take fright, we hear three extended similes about the monster's behaviour, each of eight lines.

Both *récits* in *Les Juifves* are remarkably free of such excesses. The Prophet's *récit* starts with six lines of description, setting the action in place; there is one Homeric simile of six lines (1971-76), but the other similes are of 1½ lines at most; and, despite all the opportunities for great speeches in direct speech, the words of the characters are given to us succinctly, in two or three lines of indirect speech in each case. The one area which is given a lengthy treatment is the depiction of the effect upon the spectators; and this, too, is remarkably effective in dramatic terms.

The initial description contains in its final phrase a theme which links with the ferocity of Nabuchodonosor and of the scene to come; this was the place where the Syrian kings had kept their lions, and made them fight. Immediately after this phrase the tyrant himself appears, his fury fixed with one short telling simile:

> que la fureur embrasoit au dedans,
> Comme un bûcher farci de gros charbons ardans.
>
> (1897-98)

The immediate contrast with Sédécie, who is brought on, is underlined by the three adjectives which sum him up: 'palle, maigre, hideux' (1901). There follows the only long description in the *récit*, as for six lines the other captives are described in all the detail of their misery. This has its purpose: we are presented with two completely contrasting groups facing each other, at the core of the *récit*; a dramatic tableau to which Amital, interrupting, draws our attention: 'O spectacle funebre!' (1909).

This contrast is reflected throughout the speech. Sédécie's sobs (1926-28) do not affect the tyrant, 'non plus esmeu que le cœur d'un rocher' (1937). They do, however, affect the onlookers. In two passages of six lines each (1931-36, 1947-52), we see their reactions, and their apprehension at what is going to happen. The speaker of the *récit* is affected, too, and cannot go on. This momentary heightening of the effect is followed by a resumption of the *récit*.

Sarrée is now killed, and then the other prisoners. Here the messenger lingers, with the only Homeric simile of the *récit*; he also gives us the tyrant's reaction to their desire for death. This simile, treating one of the major themes of the play, is justified in one sense, but the queens and Amital are impatient to hear what has happened to their nearest and dearest, not to linger on the fates of others; and they say so. As though to come to the point as quickly as possible, the Prophet despatches the children in three lines:

> Cela n'a du Tyran la rancœur adoucie,
> Ains forcenant plus fort, et se voulant gorger
> Du sang de vos enfans, les fait tous égorger.
>
> (1984-86)

Typically, however, he gives the full horror of it by then depicting the effect of it all on Sédécie, whose violent actions are depicted by a series of powerful verbs:

> S'outrage de ses fers, se voître contre terre,
> Et tasche à se briser le test contre une pierre:
> Rugist comme un lyon, ronge ses vestements,
> Adjure terre et ciel ...
>
> (1991-94)

Sédécie's own fate is thereafter dealt with simply, succinctly and violently. He welcomes the executioners who will bring him death:

Mais eux branlant le chef, et montrant à leur trongne
Qu'ils s'alloyent empescher à une autre besongne,
L'estendent sur le dos, la face vers les cieux,
Et luy cernent d'un fer la prunelle des yeux.

(1999-2002)

The shock of this statement requires no further elaboration. In one line the tyrant's punishment for Sédécie has become clear. The effect is startling, direct, and uncompromising. The Prophet now remains silent, as the women lament, and does not speak again until the end of the scene, 74 lines later.

The directness, and the dramatic effects, of this *récit* make it as effective, in its way, as that of Amital.

The framework which surrounds a typical *récit* contains, as Schérer points out, a series of stock formulae. The main components were usually as follows (see *32*, pp.235-39, on which this enumeration of the formulae is based).

1. The messenger appears, and bewails fate in general; he often accuses fate, too, for causing him to bring this message.
2. The hearer asks what has happened, and is quickly told the important central facts.
3. There follows an excuse for the details to be given, usually by the hearer asking for them.
4. Interruptions within the *récit* at various points.
5. The effects upon the hearers, as depicted after the *récit*.

Garnier uses the formulae, but varies them rather effectively. Amital's *récit*, of course, occurs in the middle of a conversation, so formulae 1 and 2 would be out of place; the events are distant, and known, and all that is needed is the details. These the Queen asks for: 'Comme advint vostre prise?' (689). What then happens breaks the normal pattern. Amital says she is too full of woe to speak; the Queen, instead of giving the usual encouragement to do so, does the opposite: 'Laissez donc ce propos' (691). The audience's expectations appear to be being dashed. It takes a rather convoluted few lines for Amital to say that she will in fact tell the story.

The interruption within the *récit* repeats the same trick. Usually such interruptions were either lamentations, exclamations or requests for more detailed information; and, if the speaker interrupted himself, it was to say that he could not go on, for emotion (as in the Prophet's *récit*), whereupon he was encouraged to do so by the hearers. Here Amital indeed stops because she can speak no more: 'Las! Je transis d'horreur, je forcene, j'affole,/Ce triste souvenir m'arreste la parole!' (719-20). Where, usually, the listeners would have begged the speaker to continue ('Achevez je vous pri' ...', 1955), here, again, the Queen seems to accept this as an excuse *not* to hear the *récit*: 'Ne vous adeulez pas, reprenez vos esprits,/Et relaissez plustost ce discours entrepris' (721-22). Amital is left to say that, however much it displeases her, she must continue. Again, the audience has momentarily been given the opposite message from that of a normal *récit* framework, and has been presented with the possibility that the *récit* may not take place. As with the 'genereux lion' episode, it is almost as though Garnier is playing with his audience.

Around the Prophet's *récit*, points 1, 3 and 5 of the customary framework are fairly straightforward, though the introduction of the Prophet as messenger adds a great deal of weight and importance to his introductory speech. Points 2 and 4, however, are significantly changed in order to create the maximum effect in relation to Sédécie's punishment.

The important central facts are conveyed to the listeners not in answer to their questions, but by a technique we have already seen used extensively in this play. They *overhear* his words, which are like a continuation of his opening speech. Only at line 1881 does the Prophet turn to them and address them directly. They overhear his comments and exclaim with horror and disgust.

What is significant, however, is that the death of the children, before the eyes of their father, is all that is so far conveyed. The normal purpose of the initial information at this point is, as

Schérer says, to convey the main facts to an impatient listener, before then detailing at length the circumstances (*32*, p.237). Admittedly, in some sixteenth-century plays this revelation had been left out; Garnier himself, in *Porcie*, for example, had instead accumulated horror after horror in the *récit*, with Brutus's wife in suspense ('Hé! Cassie est-il mort? ... Mais Brute, Messager, mais Brute est-il en vie? ... Et Brute vostre chef?').

Here, while Amital and the Roynes are eager to know the fate of the children, Amital is equally eager to know the fate of Sédécie. This is still kept from the audience, with the Prophet darkly commenting, when the queens call Nabuchodonosor 'le monstre infernal!' that 'il a faict pirement'. Amital cries: 'Pirement? et en quoy? las! dites-nous comment' (1890). Instead of telling her directly, the Prophet launches out into his *récit*.

During the *récit* there are several interruptions by the listeners expressing emotion at the description of Nabuchodonosor and the captives (1909-10), encouragement to continue when the Prophet wavers (1955-56), horror at the beheading of Sarrée (in the one word, 'Misericorde!', 1967), and, finally, eagerness to know about those dearest to them (after 91 lines of the *récit*).

LES ROYNES

Helas! mais nos enfans?

AMITAL

Helas! mais Sedecie? (1983)

After the three-line description of the children's death there is one more interruption of horror, and then, after Sédécie's reaction to that is described in detail, his blinding, as we have seen, comes in a swift thunderbolt, in the final line of the *récit*. Here, not only the *récit* itself, but also its framework, have been adapted to gain the maximum effect from that one line.

Garnier's use of his *récits* and their framework, then, has been aimed at an overall effect in each case. The literary and rhetorical devices within them are not there merely for their own sake, but as part of a pattern, so that each set piece is in itself a rounded, and indeed 'dramatic' work of art.

The Chorus

In humanist as in ancient tragedy, the Chorus has two roles: that of a composite character, who could take part in the dialogue, and that of a lyric interlude, dividing the acts, and indeed dividing the scenes when a change of place, or a fundamental change of personnel, was needed.

In *Les Juifves* there are two Choruses capable of performing the first role: the Chœur des Juifves and Les Roynes. For a number of reasons it is clear that the 'Chœur' at the end of each act, and in the middle of Acts II and IV, consists of the Chœur des Juifves.

Kathleen Hall has pointed out that, as in sixteenth century tragedies 'the stage represents an indeterminate place, which may from time to time change, so the Chorus can ... oscillate between individuality and universality' (*27*, p.687). The Jewish women, as a character within the acts, lament with Amital; in the 'Chœurs' outside the action they retain their characteristics as Jewish women in exile, but tend also to speak on a far more measured, general plane of general truths, often of a sententious nature. Indeed, at times they seem the mouthpiece of the religious message, commenting upon the action and the reasons for it.

So it is that the interlude-chorus draws attention to its nature as the Jewish women in the middle of Act II ('tu es cause que je pleure/Et que je sanglote d'ennuy', 289-90), at the end of Act II ('Disons adieu, mes compagnes', 815), at the end of Act III ('Comment veut-on que maintenant/Si desolees/Nous allions la flute entonnant', 1213-15), and in mid-Act IV ('En pleurs et gemissement/Nous finirons nostre vie', 1563-64). The only two interlude-choruses which do not contain this personal element are those at the end of Acts I and IV.

Those are the two choruses which contain the most general truths: the first leads on, from the Prophet's comments on the sinfulness of the Jews, to a disquisition on original sin; the second is a general chorus on Fortune. The more personal choruses, however, can also contain a stress upon important truths: the theme of idolatry as the cause of the tragedy, in mid-

Act II; sententious stanzas on how they deserve their fate, and how they must turn to God, in the latter part of the chorus at the end of Act II.

These choruses are almost entirely based on Biblical sources or Biblical themes. Among specific sources, there are the Psalms, and, in mid-Act IV (1505-64), Isaiah Chapter III. The only non-Biblical theme is the Chorus on Fortune at the end of Act IV, and even there the theme is transferred to that of God's will and power.[1]

Things are complicated, in this play, by the presence at times, from Act III onwards, of another chorus, Les Roynes. With them, until they are taken off at the end of Act IV, are their children, the children of Sédécie. These children, and their death, are an essential part of the Biblical story. The correct pathetic effect, for scenes both of farewell and grief, required their mothers, Sédécie's wives. The Chœur des Juifves would naturally be unsuitable for such a purpose.

The Chœur des Juifves, on the other hand, represents the fate of the whole Jewish nation. As such it is essential to the scene of lamentation with Amital in Act II. It is interesting, in passing, to note that in the first edition Garnier also introduced Les Roynes at this point. The restriction, in 1585, to the Chœur des Juifves seems to show that he had rightly seen the difference of role of the two groups.

The Chœur des Juifves, is, like all Renaissance choruses, present on the stage throughout the action, now a part of it, now an impartial observer from outside. Les Roynes, on the other hand, are brought on and off stage very obviously. They come on with Amital in Act III, but speak only once, right at the beginning of the scene. They participate in the scene with the Prévost in Act IV, where their concern with their children's fate is the key to their presence. They bid farewell to their children. Finally, they hear the *récit* of their children's fate in Act V, and

---

[1] The nature of Fortuna (whether she was autonomous or subject to the will of God) had been a topic for much discussion in mediaeval literature. The treatement of the theme in the Chorus to Act IV is in striking contrast to the more straightforward 'classical' treatment earlier in the play (e.g. lines 613-24), in the mouth of the 'pagan' Queen. Garnier does not, however, seem to be participating in the traditional debate; rather, he is producing the pagan version of Fortune in pagan mouths, and a Judaeo-Christian version in Jewish mouths.

break out in lamentation, before being taken off by Amital to bury the dead, thus leaving the stage free for the great Sédécie-Prophète scene. Les Roynes are a necessary part of the pathos of the play, but have no further role. The Chœur des Juifves is the perpetual observer and commentator which has the usual universal role of the Chorus.

As set pieces, the great choruses in this play are an additional weight in the scales of Biblical atmosphere, and also further supports to the version of God's aims and reasons which has been given by the Prophet. Above all, however, they are magnificent examples of lyric poetry in themselves.

4. Themes and Images

> If it live in your memory, begin at this
> line: let me see, let me see — *The rugged
> Pyrrhus, like the Hyrcanian beast* — 'tis
> not so, it begins with Pyrrhus — *The
> rugged Pyrrhus, he, whose sable arm,
> Black as his purpose ...*
> *(Hamlet,* Act II, Sc. 2)

Commonplace themes and images were an essential part of humanist tragedy, just as they were part of every other literary genre in the period. Just as there were stock epithets for Pyrrhus, so there were stock arguments for use in tragic discussions, and stock emotions to be displayed by tragic characters. Where the greatest playwrights had their greatest success, however, was in the harnessing of the expected to create the unexpected, and in the combination of stock elements to convey meanings whose significance would be clear to an audience nurtured on the conventions.

Les Juifves is possibly the richest example of such techniques. In this chapter we will be examining just a few of the major themes, and families of images, which intertwine within the play.

Acts II and III — Scenes of discussion and pleading

Scenes of discussion are the dominant feature of Acts II and III. Modern critics have tended, on the whole, to point to this feature as one of the 'weaknesses' of the play: 'L'action piétine ... Les trois discussions sur la rigueur et la clémence ne modifient jamais la volonté bien arrêtée du roi d'Assyrie, et en outre présentent des répétitions d'idées et même de termes' *(23,* p.42).

Yet it is reasonable to suppose that for a Renaissance audience these scenes must have been one of the high points of the play;

and, indeed, to a modern audience which looks at them in the same way, they can be seen to be an essential component in the well-organised shape of the 'action'.

As we have already seen, to look for 'action' in the modern sense would not be meaningful in a play such as this. The real 'action' consists of the interplay of ideas and emotions in a static context. These scenes deal with some of the major issues of the play, and prepare and prefigure the themes of the 'tragic' Acts IV and V. The fact that Nabuchodonosor does not change his mind on the need to punish Sédécie (and it is known from the start that he will not) is of no importance; the tragic outcome is already known. What can be important, however, is what the *characters* think, whether *they* believe that the outcome can be changed by their arguments.

Moreover, the very variety of these discussions creates great interest. The three protagonists, opposite Nabuchodonosor, are clearly differentiated, and the three discussions take a completely different turn from each other. Nor do they stand on their own. Themes and images are taken up from one to the other and are then echoed in the rest of the play.

Nor must one underestimate the sheer pleasure a Renaissance audience took in the details of such set pieces. We have already looked at the formal interest of the passages of stichomythia, both from the point of view of their placing and that of internal variants. Other attractions would include the 'rhetoric of persuasion', most clearly seen in Amital's scene, and also the introduction of themes of contemporary discussion.

The scene between Nabuchodonosor and Nabuzardan (205-86) misleads us from the start. Though it appears to be a stock clemency-rigour debate, it is nothing of the kind. Nabuchodonosor has already been presented to us as the stock 'tyrant'. Nabuzardan is already known to the audience historically, as his right hand man in his cruel oppression of the Jews. In the greater part of this scene, he is as keen on punishment as his master; it is the *form* of the punishment which is in question.

Nabuchodonosor's unshakeable determination to punish Sédécie is marked, here and elsewhere, by a series of oaths. Such oaths, very important to a Renaissance audience, would confirm them in their view that the outcome is inevitable: 'Mais devant que le jour ait sa course finie,/Je jure qu'il verra sa lascheté punie' (211-12). Nabuzardan does, it is true, question at first whether further punishment is needed; this gives him the opportunity to introduce the important theme of 'qualité', and of the fall of a king. This is a mere prelude, however, to the main theme of this discussion — the question of life and death.

In a dramatic half-line exchange, this theme is introduced by Nabuchodonosor punching home his determination to kill:

NABUZARDAN

Et que voulez-vous plus?

NABUCHODONOSOR

Je veux avoir sa vie.

(224)

In the ensuing discussion, both characters agree on the necessity for punishment, with Nabuzardan's *sententiae* (253-54, 259-62) bolstering up the tyrant's attitude, rather than calling for clemency. All they disagree about is the efficacity of death, with Nabuzardan holding that vengeance is lost by death, because our enemy escapes us.

Nabuchodonosor appears firm in his view. Indeed, he *appears* to swear to kill Sédécie. It would have been significant, to the contemporary audience, however, that this oath is in the conditional tense, and uses a parallel case to make the point. It shows the tyrant's firmness in the argument, but is in no way binding for the outcome of the play:

... par le Soleil je jure,
Que si mon propre enfant m'avoit faict telle injure [...]
Je le ferois mourir.   (247-51)

The theme of death as an escape, rather than a punishment, is to run right through the play. Amital's first speech, later in the act, echoes it; and, as we have already seen, the theme is, by stylistic means, made to stand out from the rest of the discussion between Amital and La Royne. All this prepares us for the 'dynamic' use of the theme in the last act.

No hint is given, here, of a change of mind in Nabuchodonosor. Nor should we expect one. The point of such arguments was for each side to makes its point with strength. Any change tends to take place between set pieces. We do later see the tyrant's position to have changed; we then look back to this scene with greater understanding.

The discussion ends with a formal and rather traditional exchange about the need for temperance even when being severe. Here Nabuzardan surprisingly takes the traditional role of the man calling for clemency; but this is complicated by the fact that this call is mainly based on the theme of 'quality'. The irony of this scene is, of course, that it is the man who is in the traditional role of 'intercessor' who has, we later realise, put into Nabuchodonosor's head his most vicious idea for punishment.

The character of the Queen, and the concern for the changeability of Fortune which she is shown to possess in her scene with Amital, makes her dialogue with her husband something very different from the Nabuchodonosor-Nabuzardan debate. The well-known affection between Nabuchodonosor and his queen has some effect on the scene, principally in the expression of the Queen's fears for her own husband's fate if he persists in his overwheening pride, but also in the King's attitude to *her*.

We have already seen the way in which the sudden break in a passage of formal and rather stock stichomythia brings out the main theme of the discussion (see p.42 above). The Queen, appalled by her husband's impiety, warns him of God's punishment of *hybris*, produces Sédécie as an awful warning of the passing nature of royal greatness, and draws the conclusion (with great overtones for the audience, who would believe her to be the same queen who speaks to Belshazzar, whom they believed to be her son) that they themselves cannot know whether their children, or even themselves, will not be brought down from greatness (929-42).

To Nabuchodonosor's 'Je n'en ay point de crainte' (943), she riposts with 'Et c'est ce qui m'en donne'. He is too arrogant;

pride comes before a fall; fear, and prudence, are more sure defenders of a crown.

Small wonder then, given the stock tyrant-figure of Nabuchodonosor, that this whole discussion is dismissed with the words: 'Laissons-là ce discours, il est plein de tristesse' (947). The Queen, undeterred, returns to the charge with further pleas for clemency. To these, suddenly, Nabuchodonosor appears to give in. His professed reason for doing so has nothing to do with the arguments; rather, it appears to reflect his adoration of the 'Median' queen: 'Pour vous gratifier je luy donne la vie:/Non qu'il ne soit puny...' (956-57). This sudden change may well satisfy the Queen. The audience's memory of the arguments advanced by Nabuzardan, and echoed by Amital, will however make them wary of the statement, and conscious of the fact that this can mean, not clemency, but added rigour. The fact that their Biblical knowledge will make them aware, at any rate, of what the outcome will be, means that their appreciation of the tyrant's irony will be lively. As though to underline this, if they have missed it, the Queen's departure from the stage enables Nabuchodonosor, in a monologue, to affirm that he *is* still a bloodthirsty tyrant, and that he *is* going to punish Sédécie even more cruelly than by death.

This monologue marks the point at which it is clear that Nabuzardan's arguments from Act II have had their effect on him. Though the tyrant's desire for vengeance remains unassuaged, the arguments *have* modified 'la volonté arrêtée du roi d'Assyrie'. It is worth noting that this is underlined by a new oath: 'Hà je jure le ciel que vostre felonnie/Sera *plus griefvement que de la mort* punie' (963-64). Typically, the full details of that punishment are not at this stage revealed.

The certainty, given by this monologue, that no pleas will change his mind, adds a certain poignancy to Amital's words as she brings the Jewish queens on stage. As the tyrant sees them, he declares that all their pleas will be 'en vain'; Amital, on the other side of the stage, is telling them that 'possible nos prieres et les cris redoublez ... attendriront son cœur: il n'est pas un rocher ...' etc. The audience, of course, knows on the basis of his oath that nothing will be changed. What is important, as always, is that the *protagonists*, or at least one of them, believe that there is room for manoeuvre.

Amital's, the longest of the scenes of argument, differs yet again from the others. In part this is once more because of the 'person' of the main protagonist, and her relation to Nabuchodonosor. She is the Queen Mother, and a person of some dignity, and age, for which Nabuchodonosor is shown as having some respect. Also she is the widow of a faithful ally of his, and makes full use of this fact; conversely, Nabuchodonosor appears to show some concern for her, while remaining implacable in relation to her son.

Above all, however, Amital's is a personal involvement. Nabuzardan's scene was basically one of cold reasoning; the Queen's, because of her fear for her own husband, takes off emotionally at one point, but her pity for the Jews is not a personal fear or anguish. Amital is pleading for her son's fate, and her people's. This scene is, moreover, a masterpiece of rhetorical attempted persuasion.

It starts with a set piece of pleading, from vanquished to victor (989-1002), in a form which had been common from the classical historians (e.g. Livy) onwards. It calls on the king, who imitates God in power, to imitate Him also in benevolence. The following discussion is on the familiar theme of the necessity for a great king to show his true greatness by magnanimity and clemency. It is also marked by the fact that Amital, far from trying to excuse Sédécie's crime, admits it fully: 'Un grand crime demande une clemence grande ... plus ce crime est grand ...' etc. (1007, 1015). Indeed it is clear that her whole approach, in the scene, is going to be based on the 'appeal to pity' rather than on any other kind of argument. When Nabuchodonosor asks her whether in justice he is right, she falls over herself to assure him that he is: 'Non, vous n'eustes pas tort, et non non, ce fut nous,/Nous mesmes de nos maux sommes cause, et non vous' (1053-54). This section of the argument ends with Nabuchodonosor's implacability causing Amital to cry out in despair, asking a question which is doubly ironic to the audience:

Hé que voulez-vous plus? estes vous implacable?
Estes vous un Tyran, un Prince inexorable?
Un homme sans pitié?   (1067-69)

The question might well be asked. Nabuchodonosor, despite
his firm defence of his right to punish, has shown Amital
civilised signs of respect, raising her from her knees after her
speech of supplication (1009). Now, in face of Amital's violent
speech (1067-78) he changes the subject abruptly, by saying that
he does forgive *her*: 'Je pardonne à vostre âge' (1079). 'Vostre
âge' here takes the place of 'pour vous gratifier' in the scene with
the Queen. He is not swayed by arguments, but by other things.

This statement opens up a new argument (1079-1109) in which
Amital calls for her own punishment. Like Seneca's Hecuba
(*Troades*, 38-40), she takes on guilt because without her the
guilty one would never have been born (1100-09).
Nabuchodonosor meanwhile has been stressing the contrast
between Amital and Sédécie ('Vous estes sans delit, mais il n'est
pas de mesmes'), and his active desire that she should not suffer
(1091, 1099).

Amital obviously decides, now, to touch on another topic
which may arouse the tyrant's sympathy: his former friendship
with her husband and herself. Her speech about her guilt ends,
tellingly, with this phrase:

                        et sans moy le colere
Ne vous forceroit d'estre envers nous sanguinaire,
Qui nous estiez ami, nous cherissant sur tous.
                                        (1107-09)

This reference to past friendship is taken up by the king: 'J'ay
tousjours bien aimé Josie vostre espoux' (1110).

This enables Amital to play emotionally on this note, firstly in
a speech detailing Josie's loyalty to Nabuchodonosor (1111-20),
then suggesting that this should wipe out all thought of
punishing his son (1122-32), then addressing her husband
directly ('O cœur vraiment Royal!/Qui fus à ton ami si
constamment loyal'), asking him to intercede for her, but in

words that are far more clearly directed at the living tyrant than at the dead husband (1133-44).

The rhetorical brilliance of these various attempts at persuasion continues even more effectively in Amital's next three speeches, which are strongly linked to each other by the techniques used. The first (1147-62), while once more admitting the gravity of Sédécie's crime, calls for equally infinite humanity for him, and stresses the danger to Nabuchodonosor's reputation ('Que diroit-on de vous?'), if he punished the children of those who were his friends; in the same speech, she calls for pity on herself, who through their loyalty to Nabuchodonosor has been widowed and deprived of her other son already. 'Par vous ... par vous ...'. It is through Nabuchodonosor that all has happened to her. Has he no pity?

The second speech, in reply to Nabuchodonosor's insistence that no-one who rebels against him should '[faire] bouclier des vertus de ses peres', is a further call for pity for herself. She asks what she has done to deserve his anger, and ironically lists the services her family had done 'pour vous ... pour vous ... pour vous ... pour vous', asking if *they* are the reasons.

In reply to Nabuchodonosor's expression of pity for her (1180-82), Amital replies, in the third of these speeches (1183-90), that it is only *he* who can change her fate. Once again, the insistent 'vous' effect is produced. If the former sufferings had been 'par vous' and 'pour vous', the decision for the future can only come 'de vous ... de vous seul'.

This whole section of the scene has been one continuous, brilliant rhetorical exercise on the part of Amital, playing on those parts of Nabuchodonosor that the others cannot reach, and in particular his apparent respect for herself. And, suddenly, the exercise appears crowned with success. The King, 'pour le respect de vous', declares that Sédécie will not be killed. Note the parallelism with the previous scene with La Royne, and at the same time the difference in his relationship with the two women, which is marked by the slight change of vocabulary. 'Pour vous gratifier je luy donne la vie' (956), 'Pour le respect de vous je luy laisse la vie' (1192).

Like La Royne, Amital is misled by this into believing that

Nabuchodonosor has been won over. This time there can be no conceivable doubt for the audience, however. They have already heard the King's monologue after his last promise; they have already heard his oath to give Sédécie a punishment worse than death. Though blinding has not yet been mentioned (and will not be, until the very final line of the *dénouement récit*), the inevitable outcome would be known to the audience from their Bible, and the ironic phrase 'Devant qu'il soit une heure il n'en verra jamais' and his promise to free the children from the yoke of servitude would send a shiver down their spine, exacerbated still further by Amital's innocent speech of happiness (1203-12).

The scenes of discussion in Acts II and III, then, fulfil an important role in terms of sixteenth-century dramaturgy. Garnier not only creates a great variety of tone and content; he also uses these scenes to rehearse some of the main issues of the play, as well as providing some superb examples of rhetorical technique.

Death and punishment

Two themes, which we have already examined, continue strongly through the rest of the play. Death as an escape, rather than as a punishment, is brought out strongly in the scene between Sédécie and Sarrée at the beginning of Act IV; Sarrée declares (1304) that all that is at stake is death, and asks what there is to fear in that; Sédécie declares he has no fear of death, which he sees as his 'port de salut'. After a discussion of Fortune, and of the causes for the punishment, Sédécie produces the heroic phrase typical of such scenes: 'Or sus, allons mourir...' (1339). Neither protagonist is aware of the unreality of this discussion, and that death is *not* the issue. As he sees Nabuchodonosor come on, Sédécie's prayer is for death:

> Fay nous cette faveur de loger nos espris
> Avec nos peres saints au celeste pourpris,
> Expiant nos forfaits par une mort severe.

(1357-59)

Nabuchodonosor's violent monologue, before he sees Sédécie, typically reminds us of the opposite. Sédécie is presumed not to hear it, so yet another ironical effect is achieved. Starting with reminiscences of yet another monologue by Atreus from *Thyestes* (176-78), this speech calls for vengeance. Its most striking lines, with a vigorous and violent repetition, talk of the death of the guilty, but then talk of the greater punishment for those who remain alive.

Ils mourront, ils mourront, et s'il en reste aucun
Que je vueille exempter du supplice commun,
Ce sera pour son mal; je ne laisseray vivre
Que ceux que je voudray plus aigrement poursuivre,
A fin qu'ils meurent vifs, et qu'ils vivent mourans,
Une presente mort tous les jours endurans.

(1365-70)

Sédécie's conviction remains that he is going to be killed, and that death is to be welcomed as a way out of suffering. At the end of the *dénouement récit*, after the death of his children, he thanks the executioners for coming to kill him:

Puis voyant les bourreaux à la hideuse face,
Teints de sang s'approcher, humblement leur rend grace
De venir terminer par une prompte mort
L'indomtable douleur qui ses entrailles mord.

(1995-98)

Brutally, in four lines, that hope is stilled.

Amital and the queens, at the news, call for death. Amital cries 'Vien, mort; vien, mort heureuse' (2009). The queens call on the tyrant to kill them.

This treatment of the theme of death is not in itself unusual; in Garnier's own *Hippolyte*, for example, Thésée is condemned to live on, and the last speech of the play is devoted to this theme, as he realises that his punishment is to live 'en langueur tant que voudront les dieux', and 'consommer quelque part mon âge malheureux', full of guilt for what he has done. What is unusual

in *Les Juifves*, however, is the way in which this theme is woven
into the whole play, from the initial discussions, through
Nabuchodonosor's ironies, to the final tragic event, and the way
in which what would otherwise be stock scenes, speeches or
sententiae are, by the insistence of the theme, given a new life
and meaning.

The death theme is purely tragic; the other most insistent
theme in the play, that of idolatry and God's punishment for it,
is a religious one. We have already seen (p.22 above, and also
20, passim) how this is hammered home, in explicit statements
by the Prophet, the Chorus, and Sédécie, as the reason for
God's anger. It continually recurs, however, in further side-
references which remind us of the theme. Nabuchodonosor is
perpetually described as an idolater; Amital, bidding farewell to
the children, warns them not to 'encenser ... aux faux Dieux des
Gentils' (1742), and 'tant que vous vivrez fuyez l'idolatrie'
(1748); in the final speech of prophecy, the return of the Jews to
Jerusalem is seen as an occasion not only for worship of God but
for rejection of 'false gods': 'Les autels fumeront de placables
hosties,/Et seront des faux Dieux nos âmes diverties' (2167-68).

As we shall see, these questions play, too, an important role in
the nexus of themes connected with Nabuchodonosor as the
instrument of God.

'God's instrument', and five related themes

As Gillian Jondorf has rightly pointed out (*22*, pp.114-17), the
problem of a 'wicked man being used by God while God remains
untainted by the wickedness of his unknowing agent' was a very
popular one with theologians and other writers in sixteenth-
century France, and one of the main examples used was usually
Nebuchadnezzar. The importance of this aspect of
Nebuchadnezzar is shown by the fact that La Porte, listing only
nine 'epithets' for him, makes one of them 'fléau de Dieu' (*30*).

Naturally, this theme therefore has to have importance in *Les
Juifves*. There is, it is true, no explicit philosophical or theological 'line' taken upon it; rather, it is used as one more nail in
the Jews' coffin of punishment, the fact that they are being

punished by someone more wicked than themselves; and moreover, as Jondorf says, there is an irony in the fact that '*Nabuchodonosor* is punishing them for *rebellion*', but '*God*, through Nabuchodonosor, is punishing them for *impiety*' (*22*, p.120).

The main questions, and answers, to this problem are raised in Act V. The Prophet, in his opening speech, rails at the barbarous king, 'execrable instrument de la rancœur celeste' (1840); he stresses, too, his impiety (1864-68). Amital, in her outburst after the *récit*, asks God to punish the tyrant, 'Bien que de ta colere il soit l'executeur' (2058). Sédécie, as he comes on blinded and in anguish, asks the crucial question: 'Je suis cause de tout, je le sçay, mais pourquoy/Me fait-il torturer par un pire que moy?' (2109-10). The Prophet then explains fully God's pattern. God *uses* the tyrant, then *punishes* him for what he has done (2113-24).

In itself, and on its own, this would be a simple treatment of a simple theme. It certainly raises, explicitly in the text, no theological complications (even if we, reading it, feel that it *should* raise some fundamental questions!). What makes this theme, and its treatment, particularly rich in literary and dramatic terms, however, is a whole nexus of themes and images, of which five in particular, in the previous acts, have built up to this scene. These themes in themselves may have been stock, or even trite; they have often seemed unconnected with each other. This last act brings all the strands together. Let us look at these strands, in Acts I-IV, before examining their later use.

1) The question of Nabuchodonosor, and his relationship with God and the gods

As we have seen, his initial 'tyrant' speech brought out his impiety as his major feature. Allusive references back to that speech abound, and emphasise the message. The first of these occurs when Amital, calling God's blessing on the Queen, says: 'En vous seule apres luy gist nostre confiance' (631). The Queen, unaware of the irony of what she is saying, ignores the mention of God as prime mover, and replies: 'Tout depend du Roy seul, nul que luy n'a puissance' (632). This clearly reflects Nabuchodonosor's view that 'Je suis l'unique Dieu de la terre où nous sommes' (193).

Amital, and Sédécie, both address Nabuchodonosor in terms which 'turn' statements from the tyrant speech, and which at times seem almost like parodies of it.

Amital's first speech of supplication to the tyrant takes up the theme of the ruler of earth paralleling the ruler of the heavens, and turns it into a plea for him to imitate God's 'bonté':

O qui, domteur du monde, avez sous vostre loy
Ce terrestre Univers, grand monarque, grand Roy,
Cheri de l'Eternel, qui de vostre exercite
Et de tous vos desseins est la seure conduite,
Comme vous l'imitez en courage indomté
Et en toute puissance, imitez sa bonté [...]
Dieu soit vostre exemplaire.

(989-94, 1006)

The statement that he owes his success to God flies directly in the face of the tyrant's arrogant views — yet it is addressed to him! Nothing could presumably have been more counter-productive.

The same passage raises another important point. This is the contrast between God and the gods. The cruel Jupiter of the tyrant speech is what Nabuchodonosor copies; God is a different kind of example. The point is made even more clearly further on in the scene:

AMITAL
Vous aurez double honneur de nous avoir desfaits
Et d'avoir, comme Dieu, pardonné nos mesfaits.
NABUCHODONOSOR
Le naturel des Dieux est de punir le vice.
AMITAL
Dieu prefere tousjours la clemence à justice.

(1025-28)

At the end of Nabuchodonosor's first remarks to Sédécie in Act

IV, he turns his impiety specifically against the Jewish God, and
his prophets, in terms of scorn which will later be of importance
to us:

> Qui t'a mis en l'esprit de faulser ta parole?
> N'en faire non plus cas que de chose frivole?
> De parjurer ta foy? seroit-ce point ton Dieu,
> Ton Dieu, qui n'a credit qu'entre le peuple Hebrieu?
> N'est-ce point ce Pontife, et ces braves Prophetes,
> Les choses predisans apres qu'elles sont faites?
>
> (1383-88)

Sédécie's 'speech of faith' is in part a reply to these insults.
There *is* only one God, all others are false (1391-98); his
prophets *have* foretold the truth, but have not been listened to
(1399-1404). Sédécie then turns to the punishment that God
metes out for such disobedience, turning his people over 'au
peuple Assyrien, Arabe, ou Philistin'; he comments that
otherwise no human force could defeat them. The relationship
to the 'tyrant' speech is pointed by the use of an actual phrase
from it. The tyrant, matching himself with Jupiter, had declared
himself to be surrounded with 'soudars indomtez' (195); Sédécie
points out that without God's help: 'encor vos soudars, bien
qu'ils soyent indomtez,/Ne nous eussent jamais comme ils ont
surmontez' (1409-10).

Of all the epithets applied to soldiers (La Porte lists 74 stock
ones), the parallelism of the adjective 'indomté' draws our
attention to the relationship between the two speeches. The
insistence on the theme of Nabuchodonosor's belief that he is
all-powerful on earth gives added strength to the prophecy, at
the end of the play, of his 'animal punishment'; for the audience
would be aware of the reason given in the Bible for that
punishment: 'till thou know that the most High ruleth in the
kingdom of men, and giveth it to whomsoever he will' (Daniel,
IV, 25).

2) Quality

Much of the argument about Sédécie's fate, in Acts II-IV, was
based on his status as a king. This subject was, as we have seen,

a popular one with Renaissance audiences.

Nabuzardan is the first to raise the question, firstly by suggesting that the worst punishment for a king is to be in slavery, and 'de Roy n'estre rien' (219-22), and then by suggesting 'que son estat à pitié vous incite' (283). The tyrant's reply is scathing: 'Pour estre Roy, sa faute est-elle plus petite?' For him, kings deserve no special treatment. Indeed, their fate should be worse, and they should be punished 'plus griefvement' (286).

Where Nabuzardan has used 'quality' as an argument for pity, Sédécie argues for his *rights* as a king, who should be exempted from punishment. '*Le devoir* vous *defend* de m'estre trop severe' (1432), he tells Nabuchodonosor, and when the tyrant speaks of the punishment he has merited, does not deny his guilt, but calmly replies: 'Vous pesez mon merite et non ma qualité' (1434). The succeeding stichomythic passage (1435-46) revolves, not around punishment, but about Sédécie's actual claim to be a king. Nabuchodonosor stresses that he made Sédécie king, that he could quite legitimately not have passed on his father's and his brother's kingdom to him, that even if he is of royal blood he is 'prince desloyal'. Sédécie's arguments are based on lineage and royal blood. The final exchange upon the subject is brutal:

SÉDÉCIE
N'aurez-vous doncque esgard à ma condition?
NABUCHODONOSOR
Je ne veux de personne avoir acception.

(1445-46)

It is interesting that Sédécie nowhere raises the question of the holy nature of an anointed king in relation to himself, though later in the scene he effectively uses it in relation to Nabuchodonosor: 'Sire, faites ainsi, vous estes en ce lieu,/Le temple, la vertu, la semblance de Dieu' (1465-66). This is the accepted Renaissance view of kingship; Garnier even uses a similar phrase in his Dedication of the plays to Henri III: 'nostre Dieu, de qui vous estes l'image et la vive representation'.

Sédécie, like Amital, is using it to persuade the tyrant to copy God: as we have seen, such arguments are useless, as his gods are not those of clemency. It will be left to the Prophet to draw the lesson of this both for Nabuchodonosor and for Sédécie.

3) Fortune and kings

This is another stock theme, central to tragedy, which we have seen treated with some richness. The Queen's concern, and Nabuchodonosor's *hybris*, have placed it at the centre of our consciousness. In Act II, in the pagan world of the Queen and of Nabuchodonosor, the theme is treated in a pagan way. In Act IV, in the mouth of the priest Sarrée, God's treatment of man is described in similar terms, with the stock reed-theme introduced into a religious statement:

> Dieu conduit toute chose, et du ciel il commande,
> Nous n'avons rien mortels qui de luy ne depende.
> Ces royales grandeurs dont on fait tant d'estat
> Luy sont comme un roseau, de qui le vent s'esbat.
>
> (1315-18)

The Chorus to Act IV similarly relates changeable Fortune to the 'Hand of God':

> Ne t'orgueillis de l'heur de ta victoire,
>   Car c'est un don de Dieu,
> Qu'il peut reprendre, et t'en ostant la gloire
>   Mettre un malheur au lieu.
>
> (1801-04)

4) Excessive suffering, and lamentation

This is a major characteristic of Renaissance tragedy. Amital, the Queens, and the Chœur des Juifves are there in order to lament. Amital stresses the excessive nature of her suffering:

> Tous les cuisants malheurs qui sur nos chefs devalent,
> Et devalerent onc, mes encombres n'égalent:
> Je suis le malheur mesme, et ne puis las! ne puis
> Souffrir plus que je souffre en mon ame d'ennuis.
>
> (367-70)

The excessive nature of Sédécie's crime is made clear not only by Nabuchodonosor ('Ton crime est excessif', 1427), but also by Amital ('sa faute est infinie', 1148); and whereas the clemency-rigour interlocutors stress that the tyrant's punishment should not be equally excessive, but that his humanity should have 'plus d'infinité' (1150), we know that Nabuchodonosor has resolved to punish Sédécie 'plus griefvement que de la mort' (964).

The idea of 'infinity' of sin and of suffering naturally leads us to expect an 'infinity' of lamentation after that suffering has been imposed. In this we shall, paradoxically, be disappointed.

5) Man and Animal

Tyrants and conquerors were, in the Renaissance, often compared with animals: 'The rugged Pyrrhus, like the Hyrcanian beast...'. Nabuchodonosor is no exception to this. In the *vituperatio* into which Sédécie breaks out in Act IV, his rage is described as 'pire que d'un lion et d'un tygre sauvage' (1484), and in the second line of Act V the Prophet makes use of one of the stock phrases from a classic vituperation: 'Qu'une Tygre felonne a porté dans son flanc' (1838).

Animal parallels abound; but the family of images connected with this takes, in *Les Juifves*, a particular turn which will be of importance to us. One of the pointers to it is the use made, at the beginning of Act III, of a speech based on a tirade from *Thyestes*.

As with the Act II tyrant speech, Garnier has taken a striking opening phrase from Seneca: 'Plagis tenetur clausa dispositis fera' (491), 'The prey is fast caught in the toils I spread'. Garnier creates, however, a far more violent and exciting effect in the speech as a whole, from the breathless repetition of the opening line onwards: 'Je le tiens je le tiens, je tiens la beste prise' (887). Such repetitions mark Nabuchodonosor's violence and impetuosity, whenever they occur ('Vous vivrez vous vivrez', 965; 'Ils mourront, ils mourront', 1365).

Seneca, however, after his opening, had turned to the actual events he was describing (referring to Thyestes and his children directly), and then produced a lengthy simile ('So when the keen Umbrian hound tracks out the prey ...'). Garnier makes the

whole thing far more immediate by suppressing the direct
references, and converting the extended simile into an extended
metaphor. Indeed, the immediacy is such that it does not even
seem like a metaphor. The repetitions of 'je' ('Je jouis ... J'ay
chassé ... J'ay ... enveloppé') make it seem that Nabuchodonosor is himself in reality the hunter. This is continued by La
Royne in the immediately following line 'Vous avez en vos mains
la proye desiree' (896). ('La proye', which can be used either in a
figurative or a realistic sense, provides here the bridge between
the powerful metaphor and the subsequent discussion of the real
situation.)

Here, Sédécie is a harmless beast, preyed upon by a man. Yet
the tyrant, in his ferocity, seems like a wild beast. This picture of
a beast-like man is underlined by the viciousness of the idea of
the victim being eaten by the hunters, with the remains being
given to the dogs: 'Que chachun ait sa part de cette
venaison./Quant au surplus je veux qu'il en soit fait curée'
(894-95).

The simple metaphor has, through the audience's awareness
of the fact that 'la proye' is in reality a man hounded by another
man, become horrifyingly indicative of the bestialisation of the
tyrant. This theme, of eating of human flesh, recurs again and
again in the play, with a variety of sources being plundered.

Some of these mentions are gratuitous additions to other
sources, such as where the description of the murder of Joachim
and the citizens of Jerusalem (431-34), based closely on
Josephus X, 97, and on the Bible, has added to it the phrase:
'Puis leurs corps massacrez fist devorer aux chiens' (434), which
does not occur in the source, but which reminds us strongly of
the fate of Jezebel (II, Kings 9, 30), and of Ahab (I, Kings 22,
38).

Then there are the examples of great stress being laid upon
one element from a related source: thus, in Amital's *récit* of the
Fall of Jerusalem, actual human cannibalism is introduced
(718), based upon a story from Josephus's account of the siege
of Jerusalem *under Titus* (Josephus, *Jewish War*, VI, 202-13,
though cannibalism was also mentioned in Ezekiel and
Jeremiah). The irony, in this speech, is that the women are

earlier described as 'plus que Lionnes fieres,/Defendant leurs petits qu'on force en leurs tanieres' (707-08). The lionesses defend their young; humans eat theirs. The lion is 'genereux' (653); human beings are as bestial as the dogs that ate Jezebel. (One man's 'venaison' is another dog's 'curée'.)

When Amital brings the queens on to beg Nabuchodonosor's mercy, the irony of her words to them is heightened by the images she uses. 'Il n'est pas un rocher', she says (977); and yet we already know that his resolution is that of a rock, and later references to him use the same image. The second image is the one that interests us here, however: 'Il n'est pas un Dragon qui se paisse de chair' (978). The epithet is an unusual one for a dragon (and does not occur in the long list presented by La Porte, *30*, p.84 vo): it is however, based on Jeremiah's description of Nebuchadnezzar:

> Nebuchadnezzar the king of Babylon hath devoured me,
> he hath crushed me, he hath made me an empty vessel,
> he hath swallowed me up like a dragon, he hath filled
> his belly with my delicates, he hath cast me out.
> (Jeremiah, 51, 34)

This reference explains the emphasis on Nebuchadnezzar's cannibalistic qualities, in this play. Garnier had found this powerful image in his Biblical source, as he had also found the theme of Nebuchadnezzar's 'animal punishment'; and this provided a nexus of themes which could underly his whole depiction of the tyrant.

Hence the dominance of the adjective 'carnacier' ('flesh-eating'), applied to him; and, in the violent dispute which is the climax of the Nabuchodonosor-Sédécie scene, the tyrant, whom Sarrée has already described as wishing to slake with their blood 'la soif de son ame cruelle' (1340), is described by Sédécie in terms which bring together the various aspects of the theme:

> Sus donc cruel Tyran, assouvi ton courage,
> Enyvre toy de sang, rempli toy de carnage:
> Là, bourreau, ne te lasse, infecte l'air de corps,

Egorge les enfans, tire le cœur des morts,
Et le mange affamé ...

(1479-83)

Je ne te crains, bourreau, carnacier, massacreur

(1493)

When Nabuchodonosor describes Sédécie's insults as being like
a dog, barking and growling, Sédécie turns this into the theme of
the flesh-eating cur:

NABUCHODONOSOR
Tu sembles un mâtin, qui abaye et qui grongne.
SÉDÉCIE
C'est toy-mesmes mâtin, qui te pais de charongne.

(1496)

A series of examples which might, in isolation, have seemed
unremarkable, and which might, if a few, have seemed merely
one facet of a variety of 'tyrant' imagery, becomes in this play
too insistent to be coincidental. This insistence gives full power
to the twist in the theme which becomes so prominent in Act V.

Act V: The Prophet draws the themes together

The whole play reaches its climax in Act V, which is
dominated by the return of the protatic figure of the Prophet,
who not only revives the atmosphere of Biblical doom, but also
ties together the major themes of the tragedy in an original and
striking way.

This process is prefigured by the last four stanzas of the
Chorus at the end of Act IV, where the Chorus turns from the
abstract Christian treatment of the theme of Fortune to certain
specific statements about the present situation: the *hybris* of
Babylon (1821-24), Babylon's lack of concern about attacking
those of royal blood (1829-32), and the sureness of God's
eventual punishment of those He has used as an instrument
(1833-36).

The Prophet opens Act V with a thunderous outburst against

the tyrant, in the stock form of the opening of a *vituperatio*, and then turns to his role as 'exécrable instrument' of God's anger. Soon he contrasts the Hebrew God with the pagan gods:

> Penses-tu qu'il y ait un Dieu dessur ta teste,
> [...] Ou bien estimes-tu
> Qu'il soit, comme tes Dieux, un bronze sans vertu?
> (1843-46)

The *reprise* of this theme is followed by the Prophet address-ing God directly, asking him to punish Nabuchodonosor. Among the examples of divine punishment he uses are some which have direct relevance to the present situation. Sennacherib (1852-54) had, like Nabuchodonosor, blasphemed against the Hebrew God, claiming that he had no power (II, Chron. 32, 15), the sons of Aaron (1857) offered 'strange fire' (Leviticus, XII), the sons of Abiram (1858) rebelled against the priesthood (Numbers, XVI). The Prophet addresses God, who has put the Israelites in the hand of Gentiles, and says that the Gentiles' mockery of God's name is 'de nos passions l'extreme passion' (1870). Finally, he points out that the tyrant thinks, arrogantly, that his victory is all *his* doing, and gives no credit to God (1871-74).

This recapitulation of a number of themes linking with Nabuchodonosor's tyrant speech, and with the other examples of his impiety, is followed by the *récit*, and its framework. Within this 'set piece' there are one or two pointers to the great final scene which is to come; of these, perhaps the most important is the Prophet's response to the lamentations of the queens: 'Ce mal est incredible, il n'a besoin de pleurs:/Les pleurs et les soupirs sont pour moindres douleurs' (1885-86).

This response to the 'infinity' of suffering prepares us in part for the great paradox of the last scene, as does the Prophet's final evocation of the excessive nature of that suffering: 'Hé Dieu quel deconfort! jamais affliction/Si estrange ne fut à filles de Sion' (2077-78).

As the Prophet sees the blinded Sédécie coming on, he draws attention, too, to the *special* nature of Sédécie's royal lineage (which is soon to be seen to be of great importance): 'Hà chose pitoyable! un Roy de la semance/Du fidelle David estre en telle souffrance!' (2087-88).

The final scene is one of remarkable impact, both emotionally and through the ideas which it expresses. The blinded king comes on, an Oedipus-figure, and bewails his fate in a series of visual images:

> *Astres*, qui sur nos chefs éternels *flamboyez*,
> *Regardez* mes tourmens, mes angoisses *voyez*,
> Mes *yeux* ne *verront* plus vostre *lumiere* belle,
> Et vous *verrez* tousjours ma passion cruelle:
> Vous me *verrez* un Roy privé de liberté,
> De royaume, d'amis, d'enfans et de *clairté*
>
> (2093-98)

This powerful speech is rounded off by a reference to the infinity and incomparability of his suffering: 'Qui vit si miserable? Autour de ceste masse/*Voyez-vous* un malheur qui mon malheur surpasse?' (2099-100).

The Prophet now interrupts him with one of the most remarkable statements of the play, brutally cutting short his lamentations: 'Non, il est infini, de semblable il n'a rien./Il en faut louer Dieu tout ainsi que d'un bien' (2101-02). There is nothing in the direct sources of this play to prepare us for this; but there is a great deal in Jewish and Christian thought. Job praised God, in his suffering: Peter called upon Christians to 'greatly rejoice, though now for a season, if need be, ye are in heaviness through manifold temptations. That the trial of your faith...though it be tried with fire, might be found unto praise and honour' (I, Peter, 6-7). Onto the classical theme of lamentation, Garnier has grafted the Christian theme of joy. Sédécie immediately responds to it: 'Tousjours soit-il benist, et que par trop d'angoisse/Jamais desesperé je ne le deconnoisse' (2103-04). He then goes on to describe his own sins, which have brought this on him, and ends merely by questioning why God has him tortured by 'un pire que moy', by a king 'qui sa grace n'invoque, ainçois qui la reboute' (2109-12).

The Prophet starts with an explanation of this, using the image of a rod used for punishment, which is then burned. God 'le souffre en ses horreurs, pour l'en punir apres'. Though He has permitted the crimes of 'ce Roy carnacier', He will avenge them, too. Babylon will be destroyed.

Sédécie welcomes this, and the fact that Babylon, by in her turn experiencing their suffering, will understand 'qu'au monde il n'est rien perdurable,/Qu'il n'y a qu'un seul Dieu qui ne soit perissable'. After thus linking, once more, the idea of 'one God' with the theme of 'Fortune', he paradoxically (after what he has endured at the hand of God) describes God as hating cruelty, and 'de carnages comblant/La maison de celuy qui ha le cœur sanglant' (2129-30).

The Prophet now launches forth into his prophecy of the future, starting with the terms used by Jeremiah ('For out of the north there cometh up a nation against her...', Jeremiah 50, 3). The imagery he uses is violent, and ends by yet again relating to the theme of drinking human blood: 'Et au sang des occis leurs chevaux abreuvant' (2142), a theme which had already been touched on, referring to Nabuchodonosor, by the queens at the end of the previous scene:

> Vien amortir ta soif dans nostre sang liquide:
> Nos enfans n'en avoyent pour te ressasier,
> Pren le nostre et le boy, nous tendons le gosier.
>
> (2036-38)

This reference leads on to the fate of Nabuchodonosor himself. The Prophet rails at him, and lists his crimes. He has profaned the temple, he has proffered blasphemies to God; both these themes are taken up from the rest of the play. A further crime is listed, however; he 'reveré n'as point/Celuy qu'il [God] a pour Roy par ses Pontifes oint'. The theme of quality, which Sédécie and Nabuzardan had discussed with Nabuchodonosor in purely temporal terms, here takes on a further aspect relating to Nabuchodonosor's impiety. Sédécie is not merely 'a king', he is 'God's anointed'. It takes the Prophet to produce this religious message; Sédécie, in Act IV, appears to have ignored it as an argument.

Nabuchodonosor's punishment is the climax of the whole family of themes we have been examining. The 'homme sanglant' will become a 'bœuf pasturant et buglant'. The viciousness of the man will become the peacefulness of the animal. From 'eating flesh' he will turn to 'eating grass'. As d'Aubigné put it in *Les Tragiques*:

> Il fut roi abruti, il n'est plus rien en somme,
> Il n'est homme ni bête et craint la bête et l'homme.

The Prophet resoundingly gives his qualifications to foretell this, in words which appear a reply to Nabuchodonosor's own scorn of the Prophets. The tyrant had described them as 'ces braves Prophetes,/Les choses predisans apres qu'elles sont faites' (1387-88). The Prophet declares: 'Dieu le veut, Dieu l'ordonne, et par moy son Prophete/Predit sa volonté devant qu'elle soit faite, (2151-52). We then have the prediction (based partly on Jeremiah and Isaiah) of the coming of Cyrus, the return of the Jews to Jerusalem; and the play ends with the prediction of the coming of Christ.

The final scene of the play has solved one of the central problems of religious tragedy: given an all-powerful God, how can the deserving be destroyed? Sédécie, despite his sins, has shown repentance. The Jews, because of their mission, cannot be completely destroyed. It takes, amid the disasters of the play, a prediction of the future, when the evil will be punished and the sins of the repentant forgiven, for a Christian message to be possible. It is in this scene that we suddenly see that most of the themes and images of the play have been geared towards that end, so that the play as a whole is seen to be a simple *exemplum* of the type which humanist tragedy tended to produce, and which in this case is a profoundly religious one.

Conclusion

It is no exaggeration to say that Garnier was the consummate master who played the instrument of humanist tragedy as it should be played. If we did not have his example before us, we would be bound to think, despite the creditable performances of a La Taille or a Montchrestien, of humanist tragedy as a lesser form than it became in his hands. Yet it was because he *used* the stock forms, not because he ignored them, that he was so successful.

Indeed, many of the brilliant effects he creates are peculiar to this poetic form. A form of 'dramatic poetry' is achieved which could not exist in any other genre. The set pieces interact, through their images and the themes they treat, rather than through the kind of dramatic progression we would normally expect; but they would fit into no other literary pattern (as Ronsard's rather weak experiments with 'dramatised' long poems show us).

Garnier succeeds not only because he is a master of dramatic verse in the sense of style (though his powerful rhythmical effects, the colour and striking nature of his imagery, etc., all go to make him so); he succeeds, too, because of his overall grasp of themes and families of images, because of his appreciation of the effects to be achieved by the placing of scenes and of set pieces and because of his sense of the overall shape for an effective play in the Renaissance mould. Above all this is spoken rhetoric of a very high order; and the oral effects within the drama are matched by static visual effects and contrasts which clearly show that performance was in the author's mind, even if reading was likely to be the predominant way in which his work might reach an audience.

Les Juifves was Garnier's masterpiece. This study has been an attempt to analyse some of the factors which contribute to its success.

Bibliography

GARNIER'S WORKS

Porcie, tragedie, Paris, 1568.
Hippolyte, tragedie, Paris, 1573.
Cornelie, tragedie, Paris, 1574.
Marc Antoine, tragedie, Paris, 1578.
La Troade, tragedie, Paris, 1579.
Antigone ou la piété, tragedie, Paris, 1580.
Bradamante, tragecomedie, Paris, 1582.
Les Juifves, tragedie, Paris, 1583.
Les Tragedies de Robert Garnier, Paris, 1585.

GENERAL WORKS ON FRENCH HUMANIST TRAGEDY

1. Charpentier, Françoise, *Pour une lecture de la tragédie humaniste: Jodelle, Garnier, Montchrestien*, Université de Saint-Etienne, 1979.
2. Faguet, Emile, *La Tragédie en France au XVIe siècle*, Paris, Fontemoing, 1883.
3. Forsyth, Elliott, *La Tragédie française de Jodelle à Corneille (1553-1640): le thème de la vengeance*, Paris, Nizet, 1962.
4. Griffiths, Richard, *The Dramatic Technique of Antoine de Montchrestien: Rhetoric and Style in French Renaissance Tragedy*, Oxford, Clarendon Press, 1970.
5. Lanson, Gustave, *Esquisse d'une histoire de la tragédie en France*, New York, Columbia U.P., 1920.
6. Lawton, H.W., *Handbook of French Renaissance Dramatic Theory*, Manchester U.P., 1949.
7. Lazard, Madeleine, *Le Théâtre en France au XVIe siècle*, Paris, P.U.F., 1980.
8. Lebègue, Raymond, *La Tragédie française de la Renaissance*, Brussels, Office de Publicité, 1944.
9. ——, *La Tragédie religieuse en France: les débuts (1514-1573)*, Paris, Champion, 1929.
10. ——, *Etudes sur le théâtre français*, t.1, Paris, Nizet, 1977.
11. Le Hir, Yves, *Les Drames bibliques de 1541 à 1600*, Grenoble, P.U.G., 1974.
12. Loukovitch, K., *L'Evolution de la tragédie religieuse classique en France*, Paris, Droz, 1933.
13. Rigal, Eugène, *De Jodelle à Molière*, Paris, Hachette, 1911.
14. Roaten, Darnell, *Structural Forms in the French Theater, 1500-1700*, Philadelphia, Pennsylvania U.P., 1960.

15. Seidmann, David, *La Bible dans les tragédies religieuses de Garnier à Montchrestien*, Paris, Nizet, 1971.
16. Stone, Jr, Donald, *French Humanist Tragedy: a Reassessment*, Manchester U.P., 1974.
17. Street, J.S., *French Sacred Drama from Bèze to Corneille*, Cambridge U.P., 1983.

BOOKS AND ARTICLES ON GARNIER

18. Barsan, Vasile C., *Garnier and Seneca*, unpublished Ph.D. thesis, Illinois, 1965.
19. Britnell, J., 'Two notes on Garnier's sources in *Les Juifves*', *French Studies* XXXIV (1980), 12-19.
20. Frankish, Clive R., 'The theme of idolatry in Garnier's *Les Juifves*', *BHR*, XXXI (1968), 65-83.
21. Gras, Maurice, *Robert Garnier, son art et sa méthode*, Geneva, Droz, 1965.
22. Jondorf, Gillian, *Robert Garnier and the Themes of Political Tragedy in the Sixteenth Century*, Cambridge U.P., 1969.
23. Lebègue, Raymond, *Les Juifves de Robert Garnier*, Paris, C.D.U., s.d.
24. Mouflard, Marie-Madeleine, *Robert Garnier, 1545-1590*, 3 vols, La Ferté-Bernard, 1961-64.

MISCELLANEOUS OTHER BOOKS AND ARTICLES QUOTED IN THIS STUDY

25. Aphthonius, *Progymnasmata* (ed. Lorichius), London 1583.
26. Du Bellay, J., *Deffense et Illustration de la langue francoyse*, Paris, Didier, 1948.
27. Hall, Kathleen M., Review of *4*, in *MLR*, July 1971, pp.686-87.
28. Josephus, *The Jewish War*, Loeb edition, London, Heinemann, 1958.
29. ——, *Jewish Antiquities*, Loeb edition, London, Heinemann, 1958.
30. La Porte, *Epithètes*, Paris, 1571.
31. Rabelais, F., *Le Quart Livre*.
32. Schérer, Jacques, *La Dramaturgie classique en France*, Paris, Nizet, 1950.
33. Seneca, *Tragedies*, Loeb edition, London, Heinemann, 1968.

CRITICAL GUIDES TO FRENCH TEXTS

edited by

Roger Little, Wolfgang van Emden, David Williams